1 LAYER DEEP

The Guide to Winning in Business
Without Losing Yourself

Praise for 1 Layer Deep

"Libby has written the rare book that actually changes how you run a business. Clear, practical, and built for entrepreneurs who want to scale with confidence. Every serious entrepreneur should read this book. Libby gives you the tools to simplify growth and build a business that lasts."

– Jonas Olson, CEO of Pest Badger

"Small business owners often believe the dream that creating systems will be the magic bullet to fix all their business problems. But most are too complicated, never used, and just waste time. The reality is, systems only work if they're simple, easy to update, and actually implemented, that's why 1 Layer Deep is different. It's practical and real-world doable, not a silver bullet fantasy."

– Jonathan Pototschnik, original co-founder of Service Autopilot

"Libby has somehow put the glory back in implementation. Do you have a fire in your business? She has the extinguisher."

– Nicole Kent, owner of Hubbard's Maid Service

"Every business needs 1 Layer Deep's playbook formula! The formula reveals how to design microplays, map out gameplans, and define roles, not people, so your company can thrive without the chaos. My mind is blown by how simple yet transformative this system is."

– Kelly Klein, owner of Tailored Home Solutions

"As a business owner coached by Libby, I've seen firsthand how these systems work. Creating an Owner's Playbook, then breaking it into smaller Gameplans and Microplays, is a true stroke of genius. This book is a game-changer for anyone who wants their team to run smoothly and successfully."

– Amy Smith, owner of Dazzle Cleaning Service

"Small, focused Microplays create big wins. Each one moves you closer to a business that runs with purpose, precision, and peace of mind."

– Ashley Russell, owner of Ashley's Dream Clean LLC

"As someone who has struggled with overthinking the traditional org chart and SOP's, the simplicity of role mapping seems divine! Pair that with the 2-Minute Rule and you can't help but have success."

– Jen Rodgers, owner of Just Peachy Clean

"This book perfectly encapsulates how tiny decisions make the overall company work better. By giving thoughtful, well documented microplays, you have an arsenal of knowledge at anyone's fingertips. Simplicity is key, and this chapter truly shows that by thoughtfully assigning individual tasks versus a whole area, can show inefficiency and help with any bottlenecks. A must read!"

– Joanne Braccio, owner of Maid To Order Fl Inc.

"Everyone said, you need playbooks! but no one could tell me how to make them. Enter 1LD - it breaks down, step by step, how to create your playbooks! This will be a game-changer for business, and home!"

– **Tami Sellers, Owner of Anchor Services Group**

"As a service-business owner, I've seen a lot of 'systems' that overcomplicate everything. This book is the opposite: one action for the result. Microplays you can write in two minutes, Gameplans your team can run, and an Owner Playbook that finally puts the right person over the right outcome. This is execution, not theory."

– **Teresa McConnell, owner of Level Up Cleaning**

"This book had me wanting to rush to the store and grab some sticky notes. It breaks down the roles and desired outcomes (microplays) in a way that can be applied to any business. Not only having a plan for accountability among team members, freeing the owners time, but a well thought out plan for any newcomer to the team! Therefore, creating a system of repeatable and successful plays."

– **Kimberly Nesselt owner of Design Your Cleaning**

"Reading 1 Layer Deep felt like Libby had literally been studying my business from the inside out & guiding me through every struggle. Every entrepreneur needs this book on their desk — it's a must-have guide to running your business with more ease, confidence and clarity."

– **Holly Silva, Co-Founder of Chores & More and The Hustle Haven**

1 LAYER DEEP

The Guide to Winning in Business Without Losing Yourself

Libby DeLucien

STONE CREST
www.stonecrestbooks.com

STONE CREST
www.stonecrestbooks.com

Stone Crest | www.stonecrestbooks.com

1 Layer Deep™ @ Copyright 2025 Libby DeLucien
By Libby DeLucien

First Edition

Published in the United States by Stone Crest Books
Stone Crest Books | www.stonecrestbooks.com
An imprint of Dinosaur House

ISBN:
978-1-961462-34-2 (paperback)
978-1-961462-35-9 (hardcover)
978-1-961462-33-5 (eBook)
978-1-961462-36-6 (audiobook)

Editor: Paul Fair
Publishing Manager: Stone Crest Books

Printed in the United States of America

DEDICATION

To Chris:

My partner, my anchor, my ride-or-die.

You found me at my absolute lowest, in my worst season, and still chose to stand by my side. You've never wavered, not just in believing in me, but in believing in the vision, the work, and the impact we're creating.

When life has felt like a hurricane, you've been my calm in the storm, the steady presence that makes the unknown feel less overwhelming.

With you, the impossible feels possible.

Here's to everything we've survived, everything we're building, and everything still ahead, together.

x

TABLE OF CONTENTS

INTRODUCTION

It was late September 2022. Hurricane Ian had been churning in the Gulf, and all the forecasts said the same thing—it was headed for Tampa or somewhere north. I was watching it closely, of course, because even if a hurricane doesn't hit us *directly* in Fort Myers, it can still shut everything around here down for a day or two. So, just in case, we started light preparation, in home, in business, and by helping employees prepare mentally and physically.

That Tuesday, I was scheduled to fly to Las Vegas to speak about what would become my 1 Layer Deep™ method. I remember dropping the kids off at my mom's house early in the morning. I told her, "Maybe I shouldn't go." But she reassured me: "It's not going to hit here. It's going to Tampa. You're good—go." So, I got on the flight.

With no direct flight, it's a long trip from Fort Myers to Vegas. By the time Chris and I landed and arrived at the hotel, the time was one a.m. in Vegas. We passed out, exhausted.

When we woke up the next morning, everything had changed. The storm had stalled overnight and strengthened into a Category Five. And now it was barreling straight toward Fort Myers. Not grazing. Not heading north. A direct hit.

And we couldn't get back.

I had left my kids, my team, my business, and I was on the other side of the country. I sat on the bed staring at my phone, watching the news, local live cams, traffic feeds—anything I could find. The water was rising. I couldn't get through to anyone. Phones went down. Live feeds went black. I couldn't see what was happening at our business or with my family. I turned to Chris and asked, "Is it too early to have a drink?" "Absolutely not," he said. "I'll get you a mimosa."

***

As a business owner, you've probably experienced moments where everything you've built is just moments from being washed away, and there's nothing you can do about it. In my case, the chaos was caused by a natural disaster. But in most cases, this anxiety-inducing, gut-wrenching "Oh no. What the Hell am I going to do now," feeling isn't usually brought on by a hurricane or a pandemic. Rather, it's a daily affliction we all suffer from, something I call an "Atlas Complex."

Atlas, one of the most well-known gods of Greek mythology, was punished by Zeus and forced to forever carry the heavens on his shoulders. In most business owners' minds, if we were to stop solving every problem our employees had, all gears would grind to a halt, and in less than twelve hours, something would catch fire and rapidly consume our entire business, leaving nothing but a pile of dust. So, to prevent this supposed catastrophe, we grind. Every day, we tell ourselves that, eventually, there will be less fires, less problems. *I can take it. One day, the load will become lighter.* The problem? While we're solving our employees' questions, complaints, and mini-fires, all the items on our Big To-Do List get pushed off to the next day. . . and the next, and the next.

Atlas was *forced* to carry the weight of the world. *You* have a choice.

Most business owners I meet are (somewhat) aware of their problem—by taking all the responsibility upon themselves, they've allowed a looming storm to threaten to sweep away their business the second their strength gives out. Sound familiar?

You probably know, in the back of your mind, that you're doing too much. You know you can only give 100 percent for so long. Eventually, your efforts just won't be enough. And simultaneously, a voice is telling you there must be a way out, a solution that will give you your business back, your sanity back, your relationships back, your time back, and even your joy back. You know this voice somehow speaks the truth, because you've seen other entrepreneurs with the life you want: owners with healthy marriages, great relationships with their kids, and a healthy diet (and let's be honest, they look pretty damn good!). These owners often start a second or even *third* business because the first is operating successfully without their minute-by-minute input. Likely, you even have a vague sort of understanding of how to achieve that: "Focus on what's important."

And that's what's most frustrating of all, to me. When I know the truth, but I don't know how to get there. In this case, there is a solution. I call it 1 Layer Deep™. It's a cross-functional method that shows you how to remove the unnecessary crushing weight your business is creating. With this method, you can follow proven steps to organize your business (and home) to achieve your dream life.

**

In this book, I will show you how to deconstruct and reconstruct your business. We'll first start by creating Microplays: small, actionable steps that answer questions, solve problems, and map issues with solutions nearly instantly for people on your team. We'll move into how to expand these Microplays into Gameplans and further into Owner Playbooks (my anti-playbook playbooks). Then, we'll show you how to cut the bull shit[1] that is stopping you (and your team) from achieving success.

An element you'll frequently encounter in this book is me—my dry sense of humor (which my husband has described as painful), my high propensity for personality and clarity over

---

[1] Yes, this book contains some swearing. I'm no Gary Vaynerchuk, but I like to use the occasional profanity for dramatic or humorous effect. If you don't like swear words, just mentally replace them with the less offensive word of your choice.

stodgy English grammar (have fun, editors), and my brutal honesty about my previous mistakes and my current learnings:

As a serial entrepreneur with three multi-million dollar businesses, I've taken not only what I've learned from the best of the best, such as Debbie Sardone, Dan Martell, and Jonathan Pototschnik, but also two decades worth of professional experience leading teams, coaching other owners, and caring for elephants (yes!), and combined them into one holistic approach to help you win at life, in both your business, and in your home. You'll read through epic wins, multi-thousand-dollar losses, and gratifying ah-ha! moments. You'll obtain the kind of knowledge one typically only gains by going through some real shit, then coming out the other side stronger, smarter, and more ready to kick-ass than ever before.

While every business is unique, owners struggle with many of the same issues. After coaching over a thousand business owners with revenues ranging from $250,000 to $10 million over the last eight years, I've found that more often than not, our problems can be boiled down to a few simple buckets and we can gain massive results from a handful of organizational tools. I've helped owners who've hired team members but can't properly train them, owners who've struggled to show up for (or pay attention to) their spouses on their weekly date night, owners who've burnt themselves out and now must fight the feelings of resentment they have toward their team and their business, and a dozen others with fractured relationships at home. No two owners had the exact same scenario, but each had been inadvertently "trapped" by their own company.

Through applying the 1 Layer Deep™ Method, owners have learned to start running their business (and, consequently, their dream life) on purpose. They start filling their days with what's right, instead of just what's loudest. They stop babysitting tasks that should have been handed off months ago. They build a leadership team that *actually* leads. They set up procedures that give them back their time—not take from it. And with clear alignment, the right intention, and bold execution, they put every tool, tactic, and principle to work exactly when it matters most.

Because the dream business (and life) you want isn't built someday. It's built today.

Pro Tip: I'll Leave Advice in Gray Boxes Like This

Many of the tactics and tools in this book are highly versatile. Not only do they work in the business world, but they can also relieve some pressure at home. I'll often drop in personal application sections that will springboard off what was previously learned about business to offer a personal-life application. I will include examples of all the ways that I've applied these principles and procedures to improve my own life. I'll also include anecdotes from myself and my clients of specific instances where it really made a big difference.

The Wake of the Storm

I closed my eyes and took a deep breath, trying to calm my racing heart. It wasn't the hundreds of people in the audience that made me nervous; I had spoken at conferences like this before. What had me worried wasn't in the crowd, it was hundreds of miles away, back home with my business. I was concerned about the horrible hurricane that was bearing down on my business, my team, and my family, everything that was important to me.

I pulled up my iPhone's news app one last time, looking for any updates. I grit my teeth as the announcer called my name. As I was giving a speech on what would become the 1 Layer Deep™ method, that framework would (hopefully) be proving itself back home.

And that framework did prove itself. Thanks to the predesigned workflows my team and family had, my family stayed safe (also thanks to our family!), and our business opened again three days after the storm. It was not all sunshine and rainbows: Our office was destroyed. We lost vehicles. Some of our employees lost their homes. I got videos from many of them standing on furniture, watching the water wash into their homes. Because of the storm and the ensuing cancellations, our business suffered a 99.8 percent loss overnight. But we recovered those clients, and more, quickly.

Looking back, I know we wouldn't have ever opened again if we hadn't reopened on that next Monday morning. And we did that, because we had procedures to follow to get us all back to work, which was a financial lifeline to many of our employees.

This is what the 1 Layer Deep™ method provided: My team didn't curl up into a ball. Instead, they executed based on preconceived procedures we'd developed in the event of a disaster. When we opened up a few days later, we knew exactly what needed to be done and who needed to do it. We had scorecards to hold us accountable. We had TikTok-sized

"Microplays" (a cornerstone of the 1 Layer Deep™ method) for everything: office procedures, team communication, customer rescheduling, and equipment-loss recovery. These weren't giant manuals collecting dust. They were bite-sized, relevant, workflows all created from lived experience and built to scale. This is what 1 Layer Deep™ provides. And it's not just a blueprint—it's a mindset.

By the time you finish this book, you'll be coming up with your own creative ways to apply this to your business, personal life, and the world around you.

PART I

THE TIKTOK OF SOPS

CHAPTER 1

Helicopter Owners

Another person was at Wendy's office door. "Hey Wendy, I was just wondering–" Wendy answered the question. Then got back to work. No sooner had her employee left than the phone rang. It was one of her field techs. Before she could answer his question, there was another knock at the door. She saw through the glass divider that there were two more of her team members, both with questions on their faces, waiting to come in. She put the field tech on hold while she gave each of the team members an answer and then answered the field tech's question. *Why are there **so many questions?*** Wendy took a deep breath and got back to work. Her computer dinged. Her email inbox was now full. It wasn't even noon.

Over the last few months, Wendy's team had tirelessly questioned her about everything. She hadn't even touched the budgeting report she needed to review, the new-hire resumes she needed to handle, or the blogpost she'd been working on. She had just been trying to keep daily operations running. She desperately needed a break, but she knew she couldn't go on vacation—if she even left for a weekend, everything would fall to pieces. She was trapped in a business that she was growing to hate.

Most of us entrepreneurs have been in a similar position as Wendy. The questions just keep coming. We are stuck putting out fires with no time to work on what we are truly passionate about—growing our business. We're replying to the same emails over and over again: "Use the business card for this." "Here's how you onboard a customer." "The form you're looking for is right here." "Here's how to manage this particular client." We're handling payroll, taxes, and accounting. We're helping sales, assisting marketing, and keeping customers happy. . . all while watching the "hustle, hustle, hustle" social media content that half of the internet is putting out. Of course, the *other* half is snapping photos of their yachts and fancy cars, which is why it's easy to fall into the trap of believing that there is an oasis just around the corner. *If I work hard enough, long enough, then it will all pay off.*

Dan Martell, author of *Buy Back Your Time,* commonly refers to this trap as the "GSD mentality,"[2] an errant philosophy in which entrepreneurs think that if we just Get Shit Done, eventually we'll find the freedom we deserve. So, we hover over everything in our companies, micro-managing, never finding a break, never allowing anyone else to take the reins and execute. Sure, we may hire someone to do a task—say sales or marketing—but we never *let go.* The mental burden stays firmly on us, the owners.

A "helicopter parent" is one who hovers over their kids, protecting them from all bumps, bruises, and learning experiences. Unintentionally, helicopter parents are inhibiting their children's growth, and in that scenario, kids fail to learn how to function autonomously. Much in the same way, a helicopter *owner* never allows those in their business to grow into their full potential. These

---

[2] Dan Martell, *Buy Back Your Time: Get Unstuck, Reclaim Your Freedom, and Build Your Empire* (New York: Portfolio/Penguin, 2023).

entrepreneurs keep all of the answers and information in their heads, not putting any of it down on paper or in an accessible place, so they never relieve themselves of any of the pressure. Often, the helicopter owner stands behind their employees, fixing all their problems and answering all their questions (no matter how many times the question has already been asked). Not sure if that's you? Ask yourself this:

How long could I go on vacation and feel comfortable leaving my employees to run my business without me?

If you're like most business owners I coach, the thought of vacation immediately makes you think, *How will **anything** get done right without me?!* If that was your gut response, guess what? You're a helicopter owner.

Here's the simple truth: It's not your employees' fault that they keep coming to you for the same questions, over and over again. It's not their fault that you're the linchpin of your entire organization. And it's not their fault you're stressed, but it *does* make sense: You're one gear in a growing company, and right now, all the stress is on that one gear. Eventually, it's going to break.

If you're thinking, *How will <u>anything</u> get done right without me?!* Guess what? You're a helicopter owner.

The trick to removing the focused stress on this one gear is simple: remove *yourself.*

In his book *Atomic Habits*, James Clear writes that "you don't rise to the level of your goals, [but rather] you fall to the level of your systems."[3] I have a twist on this, one that applies to businesses:

> **Your people are only as good as your processes.**

Sure, if you own a roofing company, each roofer may know the goal is to "put up roofs," but do they know your specific procedures for clean-up? Do they know who's responsible for the final sign-off? Do they know where to park their car, when or if to put a sign in the yard, or how to collect payments?

If you're feeling like Wendy, I bet I could ask each of your employees, right now, who they are supposed to go to when they have a question. My guess is, they'd shrug and point to you, which they'd do because the "procedures" most owners develop all point back to them. Our employees don't know where to find the answer on their own, what power they have to solve a problem, or who to ask (other than you or me) when they don't know the answer. With no Playbook other than "ask the owner," they're basically acting within company policy.

Eventually, I had a key revelation, one that's hard for

---

[3] James Clear, *Atomic Habits: An Easy & Proven Way to Build Good Habits & Break Bad Ones* (Solon, OH: Playaway, 2023).

entrepreneurs to accept because us founders are, by nature, wired for risk. But *employees* crave stability. They need to know that there is a right way to do something, and they need to know what that right way is. (Indeed, the most valuable feedback I have ever received from an employee is that they need to know when they're doing something right.) Without an objective metric or desired outcome, employees lose their sense of accomplishment and purpose, which can lead to resentment and insecurity. That's on their side. On *your* side, you'll be frustrated because they'll never do things to your standard (because you don't have one) and they'll never know which procedures to use (because there aren't any).

On the flip side, imagine if your team knew. . .

- *What* to do, when to do it, and how to do it.
- *Where* to find the answers to common questions. ("What do I do if a customer pays late?")
- *Who* to ask when they really can't find the answer.

The key is having those three elements covered without your daily involvement. Here's what I've painstakingly learned that solves all three:

1. Microplays that give bite-sized instructions and standardized procedures for each task
2. A place to find all necessary information

The foundation is getting the right information to the right person in the right way at the right time. Many businesses call these "standard operating procedures," "SOPs," or "Playbooks." I have a different spin on this idea, one that I call *Microplays*, and we'll get into that later. Regardless, the key is having *some sort* of documented standard and some sort of methodology for reaching that standard. Then, of course, that documentation needs to be accessible by your team.

"But I've *tried* to make standard operating procedures before, and no one uses them, Libby!"

> **The foundation is getting the right information to the right person in the right way at the right time.**

I hear this all the time. Some owners, like Wendy at first, have *no* standard operating procedures, and they've never thought about making them. Others have spent hours creating elaborate standard operating procedures, only to find that no one uses them outside of initial training. If that's you, again, the problem is *not* your staff. The issue is simple—you didn't create those standard operating procedures with *your employees* in mind. You likely created standard operating procedures for the owner (you) and developed them in line with how *you* think and how *you* would use them.

The Unhelpful SOPs

Often, after an entrepreneur hears about the importance of standard operating procedures from a colleague, they go online and start creating folders (likely in Google Drive) around the core "departments" of their business. They'll usually create three to ten top-level folders for each, with names like "Sales," "Marketing," "Employees," "Finance," and "Customers." Then, under each of those folders, they'll create the necessary sub-folders, such as "Front of House" or "Taxes." Then, under those, they create sub-sub-folders such as, "Training Videos" or "1099s." And then, of course, under those you often find. . . sub-sub-*sub*-folders like "SOPs for Year 2020" or (my personal favorite) "Miscellaneous SOPs."

Now, think through the process here: Unless an employee is in training, they aren't going online randomly to look for standard operating procedures. If an employee who's been at your company for longer than six months were to ever look for a standard operating procedure, they would only do so because:

- A) They're trying to find something to put them to sleep, or
- B) They have an *immediate* problem they want solved

Take Miri. Miri's a new hire at a mom-and-pop coffee shop. One day, the credit card reader stops working. She has a line of customers. "What do I do?" she whispers to her co-worker, Zack, who's worked there for longer. He stops making drinks to show Miri how to reset the machine. People in the growing line start to get fidgety. The credit card machine comes back on, but it's still not working. Zack and Miri look at each other with panic on their faces, *What do we do now?*

Like most employees in this situation, Zack and Miri know exactly what to do in a situation like this, which is, in fact, what to do for nearly every situation: call the manager. The manager, Ashley, comes over. She tinkers with the device, before calling *her* boss, the owner.

Now, Zack, Miri, and Ashley are all on a FaceTime call with the owner - who's on vacation - trying to walk them through how to reset the Wi-Fi, clear the browser on the connected iPad, and re-log-in into their payment processor. By now, the line is *shrinking* as customers have become increasingly frustrated.[4]

Now, the owner may have had that procedure very well-documented. Likely, the only thing her employees had to do was, go online to the company Google Driver folder called "Local Coffee Shop," then choose "Front of House," then click on "Day-to-Day Ops," then skip "Old POS" and click on the folder titled "New POS," then find "Emergencies," then find "Reset the System" then start over and look for another file that's under "Local Coffee Shop" then "Front of House" then "Login Information" then "Login Information

---

[4] By the way, this is based on a scenario my team witnessed while doing research for this book!

2025" then "Passwords." Then, put it all together. Piece of cake.

That's the problem with how most entrepreneurs make standard operating procedures. They develop a multi-layered system that usually has about five (I've seen *ten)* layers between the employee's question and the answer. And at every step along the way, the employee must have memorized which folder to choose amidst multiple options, all of which have vague titles and funny acronyms. That's if everything is filed and titled *accurately.* Throw in a couple misplaced files, and there's about a negative 10 percent chance an employee can find the answer they need in a minor emergency. So, they call you. Their own, personal, workplace ChatGPT.

The Unfriendly Search Feature

Yes: Many virtual filing systems (such as Microsoft Drive and Google Drive) have added a search feature. The problem is, again, most standard operating procedures aren't created for *how the* **employee** is going to use them. Don't believe me? Try this: If you have a Google Drive with all your company's standard operating procedures, go online right now, and try to find what an employee should do with an upset customer who wants a refund. I'm going to guess that's not documented anywhere that's less than forty-seven-and-a-half-folders deep under a pile of old information. Now, try to use the search feature. Put in "upset customer." How did that go? What about "refund"? Any results? What about "customer" . . . how many results are there on that one? (I tried this with one partner, and there were *hundreds* of results for "customer," but few for the others, none of which answered the question.)

That's why your employees can't find the answers to their questions: they don't have the time and energy to sort through your "here's-how-I-like-to-organize-folders" insanity. (And again, that's if you have anything documented at all. Most business owners don't.)

We'll get more into the *how* in the coming chapters. But for now, I want you to wrap your head around this question:

What if it were easier for someone to find the information they needed than to ask me for it?

That's what 1 Layer Deep™ is all about. It's about cutting through B.S. and getting down-and-dirty with what's needed. It's about putting the information and the tools at the fingertips of those who need it most.

That's what I'm going to show you how to do, in the simplest way possible.

Don't believe me? Ask Wendy.

Where Wendy Is Now

Before Wendy organized her business, she was exhausted from answering questions and solving her team's problems.

She had forgotten why she started her business in the first place. She fell out of love with her business and even began to hate it. She had no idea what to do. And that's when she found what I now call the 1 Layer Deep™ method. She decided to put in the effort up front so that she could reap the rewards. She documented everything down to the smallest detail: passwords and usernames, procedures, roles, and responsibilities. She made Microplay after Microplay for any task she could think of. She created and defined the roles in her company. Along the way, she realized that any organizational system is a living thing, one that would need to evolve to fit the needs of the company, and some workflows and Microplays would fall along the wayside, and new ones would take their place, while others remained unchanged.

After lots of hard work, Wendy's business has transformed. In her small town with a population of about 5,000, she has tripled her revenue from half a million to over $1.5 million a year. She has created an environment that not only sets herself up for success but has set up her entire team and business for success. Today, Wendy will tell you that the single most important thing she did was apply the 1 Layer Deep™ method to *everything*.

And that's what it is—a mindset, not just a framework. Sure, in this book, I'm going to provide you with tons of practical ways to apply this method, but what I really want for you is to let the overall *mindset* of 1 Layer Deep™ worm into your mind: It's all about eliminating friction between a person and their desired outcome. It's about reducing the necessary steps from 947 to *one*. While in this book we'll be focused primarily on creating workflows for your business, you can apply this methodology to anything, right here, and right now. Simply ask yourself the 1 Layer Deep™ ultimate question: *How can I eliminate everything in this process except the one step that's truly necessary?*

The 1 Layer Deep™ ultimate question: *How can I eliminate everything in this process except the one step that's truly necessary?*

Are your clients struggling to pay invoices on time? Reduce the friction to *only one button* before your customers can put in their credit card number.

Does your spouse struggle to say and do what you want? Write down a list of words you love to hear, places you like to go, and foods you love to eat. Then, tape it to the bathroom mirror where they brush their teeth.

Most importantly for our purposes. . .

Are your employees asking *the same questions over and over again?* Make a list of the ten questions you've answered more times than "Are we there yet?" and put them in a document at the very top of your company portal and call it "0.0: Frequently asked questions." [5]

---

[5] Most alphabetically organized systems will put "0.0" at the very top, before "A."

Change the Process, Change Your Business

A colleague of mine, Alex Duta, likes to mention that you only have a few levers in your business, and they mostly start with P. For instance, two of the biggest are your *process* and your *people*. Those levers can be changed to revolutionize your business. And here's the truth:

Until you fix the process, it won't help to change your people. And if you fix the process, you often won't *need* to change the people. If you can get to the root of your process problems, fix them, then you can not only go on that vacation, but you can also grow your business, and change more lives. You just need to give everyone around you a way to find the information they need *without* talking only to you. Stop being a helicopter owner, right now, and start thinking *1. Layer. Deep.*

ΛΛΛ

CHAPTER 2

1 Layer Deep™

The $300 Million Button

In 2009, Jared Spool, a user experience expert, was hired to solve a company's problem: customers would shop their site, adding items to their carts and then go to check out.[6] The problem was, a high percentage of people who reached that point would end up abandoning their cart. So, the company put Spool on the case. After some polling and digging, he found that there was a common complaint with the majority of shoppers: they didn't want to register. When they got to the checkout page, they were given the option to login or register to complete the purchase. The site was asking for

---

[6] Jared M. Spool, "The $300 Million Button," UX Articles by Center Centre, June 11, 2021, https://articles.centercentre.com/three_hund_million_button/.

things that they would need to ship the products either way, but something about the word *register* turned potential customers away. Spool made one small change. He left the log in button alone, but he changed the register button into a "continue" button, along with the message: "*You do not need to create an account to make purchases on our site. Simply click Continue to proceed to checkout. To make your future purchases even faster, you can create an account during checkout.*"

This simple change, moving the title from "register" to "continue," resulted in massive boosts in sales for the company. In fact, with the change of a single button, Spool made the company an extra *$300 million.*

That's the cost of the friction, the cost of extra layers. People were so disheartened at even the *thought* of having to go to another screen to register, they were spending millions less on their shopping. They'd rather hop in their car and drive all the way to a store, or spend time on another website, then go through what they thought was going to be additional layers of hassle. Logical? Maybe not. But let's stop fighting against human psychology and work with it. The truth is, people will do whatever they even *perceive* to be the most frictionless way forward. By making the button say "continue" (without changing anything other than the title), people felt at ease to move on. That feels 1 Layer Deep™.

Now, in this book, we're going to move beyond feeling and move on to reality. We're not only going to remove the negative feelings associated with friction, but we're going to remove the unnecessary layers themselves.

And that's what the 1 Layer Deep™ method is all about. . . it's about having the information 1 Layer Deep™ so that others (namely, employees) will go to that place to find the answer.

Today, app creators know this premise of friction all too well—software companies will spend thousands or millions on research and testing to make their apps and screens easier and easier and *easier* to navigate so that users will stay on their system. Instagram? You log in *and immediately scroll.* Apple Maps on your iPhone? Log in, and the address field is already there, so you only had to click *one* thing, the app icon. Go to Google.com, and the search bar is right on top, and you can start typing (again, you had to go to *one* home screen to get to the search feature). All these applications are applying a 1 Layer Deep™ mindset, even if they don't call it that: they've all developed products that only require one interaction between a user and the outcome they're looking for.

> **The 1 Layer Deep™ method: There should only be one action required before the desired result.**

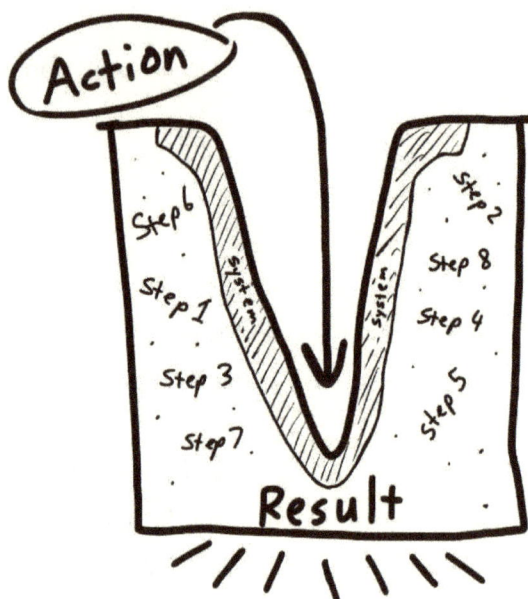

The truth is, people are only willing to take exactly one action to find the answer (or solution) they need. Right now, you are *already* applying this 1 Layer Deep™ mindset in your business. Guess what the one layer is that you've created *at your business*? It's you. You're the layer. You're the one step that people take to get to the desired outcome.

- When Zack, Miri, and Ashley can't get the credit card reader back on at your coffee shop, they call you.
- When a client is upset and asks for a refund, your account manager calls you.
- When someone wants to know your company's maternity leave policy, they call you.

One question, and the answer's solved. You've done a fantastic job of making *you* the easiest and simplest way to get information.

Let's go back to the coffee shop example from the previous chapter (Remember, Miri's working at a coffee shop when the register freezes up, then she asks Zack to help, who asks the manager, who calls the owner). In a nutshell, 1 Layer Deep™ would have simply suggested that instead of Miri whispering to Zack to ask Ashley to FaceTime the owner, Miri would simply have gone to the company portal and looked for her exact problem, labeled, and called out exactly like this:

"I'm trying to take a payment, and the credit card processor has gone down."

If a file were labeled exactly like that and it were easily findable, why wouldn't Ashley, Zack, or Miri use it?

When your account manager wants to know how to deal with an angry, upset customer, with 1 Layer Deep™, they'd go to the same company portal that Miri used, and simply look for, "I'm talking with an upset customer, and they want a refund."

Your new employee who wants parental leave would find the file that reads, "I need time off work, and I don't know how to request it." [7]

---

[7] I know what you're thinking: *There's no way I can have EVERY question listed out.* Actually, I've solved all this for you, after *years* of figuring out human and employee-psychology. Keep reading!

What if you never had to answer these (and other) basic questions that you're getting asked over and over again, because they were all listed out exactly one layer away from your employees? What if all *related* questions were also housed in the same place? What if everything your employees wanted to know was so easy to find, and so well-documented that finding the answer to almost anything and fixing nearly any problem was *simpler and faster* than getting a hold of you? Here's how you do that:

1 Layer Deep™ Methodology

In the basic framework of 1 Layer Deep™, there are three steps:

- Align (Determine what the intention of the user (customer, employee, etc.) is)
- Delete (Remove the other layers, or, as I say, "Cut the B.S.")
- Execute (Get the end user all the way to that final step, so they have *only one step* to take)

These three pieces, Align, Delete, and Execute, are the groundwork for everything that 1 Layer Deep™ does; apply them systematically and we can make any process more efficient and effective.

But don't leave it simply as a business framework. It's also a **mindset practice**. We use two sets of questions and statements to keep ourselves clear when we're thinking about customers and our own personal lives.

External Application (customers, team, family):

- Alignment: *What does ____ really NEED right now?*
- Intention: Cut the B.S.
- Execution: Do the Hard Thing
- **Get What They Need**

Internal Application (self-reflection):

- Alignment: *What do I really WANT right now?*
- Intention: Cut the B.S.
- Execution: Do the Hard Thing
- **Get What You Want**

This is where the framework comes alive. For example:

- *What does my daughter really NEED right now?* Cut the B.S. It's not what I WANT, it's what she NEEDS. Do the hard thing. Then she gets what she needs.
- *What does sales really NEED right now to close more leads?* Cut the B.S. The team isn't failing; they just don't have warm leads. Do the hard thing and fix the lead source. Then they get what they need.

Start practicing 1 Layer Deep™ both ways. **Align, Delete, Execute** on the business side, and Alignment, Intention, Execution for these **External/Internal phrases** on the mindset side. You'll gain incredible clarity and efficiency in your company and in your daily decisions.

Align ⟶ What do you REALLY want?

Delete ⟶ 💩 Cut the B.S. ✂

Execute ⟶ Do the hard thing

✨ Get what you want ✨

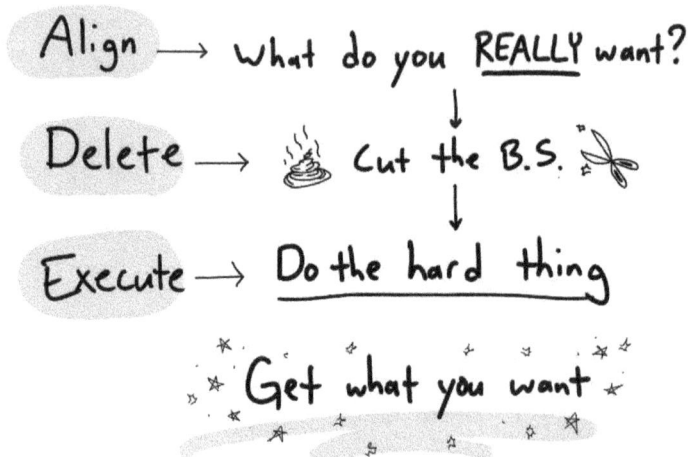

This is essentially what Spool did with his $300 million button-title change:

He aligned on what the users wanted (to *not* have to fill out extra information). He then removed all the emotional layers by changing the title to Continue (delete), then allowed the users to get to their goal by simply clicking that button and moving on (execute). Similarly, the app creators do the same: They find what users are wanting, whether that's to scroll content or find directions (align), then, they cut out all the B.S. by *deleting* any unnecessary screens or steps. Then, they put that one action up at the front. Execute.

This can be done in small and large scales. For instance, we want to apply this Align-Delete-Execute with questions being asked of our team. If employees are often coming to you with questions such as, "How do I request time off?" we don't want them having to go through layers of answers to get to that solution. Instead, we want to create a solution that answers that specific question with "Here's how you request time off." If you want your employees to go into work and clock in *immediately,* you can make a simple change, and move the clock-in right next to the door as they come in. In that way, you would have aligned you and your team with the expectations that you want (to clock in immediately), deleted the (literal) additional steps it was taking them to get to the clock-in station, and then, allowed them to easily execute that task.

Those are small-scale ways of applying this Align-Delete-Execute idea.

But it shows up in larger ways throughout your organization—you may need to re-align your entire company around financial objectives that seem to have been forgotten. You may need to then delete some extraneous projects that are distracting from that goal. Finally, you'll need to execute to achieve.

There's a legendary story about the man Walt Disney that occurred before he finished construction on Disneyland. Walt knew that, at the time, theme parks were little more than trash-ridden carnivals. And he wanted *his* park to be immaculate. So, according to legend, he went to nearby playgrounds and public spaces then counted the number of steps people were willing to take before they got to a trash can. He found that people would throw their trash on the ground if they couldn't get to a trash can within seven steps. Today, I dare you to go to any Disney theme park and try to go more than seven steps without finding a trash can. It's impossible.

Walt applied Align-Delete-Execute across entire theme parks to achieve cleanness. You can do the same to achieve streamlined efficiency. Here are the basic steps involved:

1: Align

In this step, evaluate what you are actually trying to achieve in a given situation. What's the aim? Sometimes, this is as simple as moving the clock-in closer to the door. Other times, this may require hard conversations and honesty with your team, but this pursuit of unity is essential for the success of the business. If you and your team aren't all bent on the same goal - or if you've never told them what the goal actually is - it's going to be that much harder to achieve a desirable outcome.

2: Delete

Next, we need to streamline the journey to the desired outcome. Chances are you spend much of your time trying to optimize your business. Sometimes, that's part of the problem. Elon Musk once noted that one of the biggest traps for *smart* engineers is to optimize that which shouldn't exist.[8]

---

[8] Tim Dodd and Elon Musk, other, *Everyday Astronaut*, n.d., accessed 2025

This applies perfectly to our businesses. Most people think of optimization like making things better at what they do, but that's not true optimization. Real, honest efficiency is reaching the goal faster with less friction. Sometimes that looks like improving and streamlining them, but more often than not, it really looks like cutting out steps altogether (like the three chapters of this book that didn't make the cut!). Cut out the extra steps, the extra clicks, and the extra work. "Cut the B.S."

When dealing with employee questions (which we'll solve in the next chapter, once and for all), the B.S. is usually extra, unnecessary steps. But when I'm coaching owners on higher-level problems, often the B.S. that I'm cutting out isn't tangible. It's emotional, it's ego. In Chapter 7, I'm going to show you how my dear husband once had to deal with this. Once we aligned, he realized the B.S. he would need to cut out was his ego, and until that happened, he wouldn't have been able to grow as a person or as a leader. Similarly, In the story of the $300 million-button, what was holding the customers back was psychological barriers. Even after Spool changed the title, customers \ still had to fill in the same information to purchase their items. Spool didn't decrease the work they had to do. The thing that was holding them back was their perception of the process. Even though the process was simple, it was not 1 Layer Deep™ because it carried the psychological baggage of a much longer process. Sometimes cutting out the B.S. means tearing down the mental barriers.

Now, before we move on to executing the new process (step three), we need to reevaluate. We need to go back to Step 1: Align and ensure our priorities are still the same. Often, after cutting out B.S., we realize that the goals have slightly shifted.

I was working with a company that thought the problem was simple: we just need more applicants. So that's where we started. But once we started cutting the B.S., it became clear that wasn't the real problem at all.

The bottleneck was the screener. Instead of making candidates excited about the job, they were dragging the process out and making it feel like a chore. They weren't selling the opportunity, so good people were dropping out before they ever made it to the company.

At that point, it didn't matter how many applicants we brought in—the process was broken. So, we had to go back to Step One: Align. The goal wasn't "get more applicants." The goal was "fix the screener," whether that meant retrain, reassign, or replace. Once we fixed that choke point, then execution made sense.

This is pretty common with complex problems: First you Align, then you begin to Delete (cut the B.S.), and as you start cutting, you must often realign your initial goals. Repeat, until the goal of execution becomes crystal clear.

3: Execute

Finally, it's time to execute. It's time to buckle down, do the hard thing, and follow through with the changes you've planned. If all you had to do was move the clock-in station up to the front of the building, execution may not be difficult. But if Execute is "fire my COO," this may be more difficult.

In the next chapter, we're going to discuss Microplays, or, how do you get your employee to the answer they want in one click, so they stop asking you. In this case, "execute," means *you* must do the hard work of thinking for your employee, so you've thought through all the steps so well, so that your employee now just has one action to take to execute. In that case, *that's* the hard thing.

Execute often implies a layer of difficulty, sometimes, it's thinking, sometimes it's working through emotional or psychological pain, but regardless, it's necessary to ensure that 1 Layer Deep™ is preserved.

***

Now, if you're thinking *Libby, I don't care about your Align-Delete-Execute idea. I want my employees to stop asking me silly questions.*

Well, in the next chapter, we're going to end that once and for all.

1 Layer Deep™ Personal Application

Stop Maximizing Your Weaknesses

If we're to cut through the B.S. in our, a great place to start is with ourselves.

Some people might feel the urge to disregard this section. I strongly encourage you not to. In psychologist Jordan Peterson's book *12 Rules: An Antidote to Chaos*,[9] his second rule is "Treat yourself like someone you are responsible for helping." Peterson discusses a paradoxical phenomenon: people are far more likely to fill a pet's medical prescription than their own. We tend to disregard our own needs, especially when they are competing with someone else's. While this seems selfless, it also has its dark side. By neglecting ourselves, we are keeping ourselves from being able to do our best for others. Think of the message that airlines give before takeoff: "If the cabin loses pressure, oxygen masks will drop from the overhead panel. Put on your own mask before assisting others." Ideally, everyone puts their own mask on, and everyone is safe. Of course, we all know not everyone will be able to help themselves. But if the plane starts going down and you start trying to help someone

---

[9] Jordan B. Peterson, Ethan Van Sciver, and Norman Doidge, *12 Rules for Life: An Antidote to Chaos* (Toronto: Random House Canada, 2018).

else put their mask on, chances are you'll pass out before you're able to fully assist them. Then everyone is out of luck. Similarly, in life, you can't deal with others' problems until we've dealt with our own.

What does this look like in practice? The easy answer is to "focus on our weaknesses." But that's vague, and an obsession with our own weaknesses leads to frustration. Personally, I wish I could have back all the time I've spent trying to grind away at my flaws. My counterproposal is simple: minimize your weaknesses and maximize your strengths.

We must find ways to *beat* our weaknesses. Often, we pour resources into trying to train or practice away our weaknesses. Instead, we should minimize the impact they have. Picture a chess game where the king finds out he is vulnerable to multiple pieces, and then, he immediately moves out into the middle of the board unprotected so that he can "get tougher" or "deal with his weaknesses." Ridiculous. But how many of us have tried that very strategy? Our job isn't to go on the offensive, particularly in the areas where we're most weak. Instead, we should learn to minimize our weaknesses and delegate to someone's strength.

For instance, if I have a set of tasks that I'm really not looking forward to, instead of trying to "power through," I'll call my assistant and tell her to hold me accountable. Admitting to myself that I need her help is a big part of the process. Sometimes that even means jumping on a call together for accountability, because I know I'll keep pushing it off otherwise. Sometimes, she'll tell me to take a break. Other times, she'll tell me to get to it. Either way, instead of trying to just muscle through, or, on the other end, pretend as if I *don't* have those weaknesses, I've learned just to minimize the impact. Accountability is a great tool there

Imagine a fish that learned it couldn't run as well as a cheetah, and while all the other fish were getting better at swimming, this fish scraped its fins across the ocean floor, trying to run as the cheetah does. If that fish were to ever go on land, it would lose the cheetah, despite its silly practice sessions across the ocean floor. That's how many of us look when we throw ourselves into situations that exploit our weaknesses and don't cater to our strengths.

By knowing our strengths and weaknesses, we are empowered to lead our businesses. Take advantage where you can, and avoid situations where your weaknesses are exposed (it can also be super helpful to hire help in those areas of weakness).

***

In *Atomic Habits*, *New York Times*-bestselling author James Clear talks about Michael Phelps and Hicham El Guerrouj.[10] Phelps's towering six-foot-four frame makes him the ideal swimmer, while shorter El Guerrouj is built perfectly for his sport—middle-distance running, where he's collected a slew

---

[10] Clear, *Atomic Habits*

of Olympic and world championship medals, and, as of 2025, ad still holds world records in the 1500 meter and the mile. Both are elite athletes. Both train hard. Both are talented. But a major contributor to their individual success is the fact that they both picked a sport to which they are suited. If they swapped, both could train just as hard, and neither would qualify for the Olympics. We are all predisposed to have advantages in certain arenas. To be truly successful, all we must do is find the arenas we excel in and take full advantage of them. The same principle applies to those around you as well—your employees, your team, and your family.

CHAPTER 3

The Ten (Micro)Plays Every Business Owner Needs Yesterday

Playbooks are dead.

At least the playbooks that you're used to.

Pages-long documents of corporate legalese detailing all the ways *not* to do something. Dusty, dismal, and in disuse; no one has found them relevant or helpful. . . ever. The problem with these playbooks isn't the idea itself; having a standardized (and documented) workflow is a great idea. The problem is the form that the information takes.

When our employees ask us questions about tasks, they're not asking for a long, drawn-out exposition of all the things to watch out for; they're asking for instruction to accomplish a specific, typically immediate, goal. They're asking for tools that will help them get the job done, and not a word more. That's where Microplays come in. Microplays cut through all the B.S. and give the employees exactly what they need to do the job and do it right in the way they need it most. With the old, lengthy Playbooks, your employees had to search through all the nonsense to find the information they needed. Or worse, they avoid the standard operating procedures altogether. Microplays eliminate both situations: they are so easy for employees to access and so easy for them to use that they will start to see them as tools instead of homework.

And these Microplays are the heartbeat of the 1 Layer Deep™ method: they provide the most basic unit, the quickest way to put the system into action, and you'll have the most important ones within the next ten minutes.

"Where's the Restroom?"

When you go through training for nearly any position at a Disney theme park—whether to be a character attendant, a hot dog seller, or a custodian—you'll likely hear them tell you this: part of your role is to always know the location for the nearest restroom. Because no matter what, *someone* is going to ask you, "Where's the bathroom?" Similarly, there are questions in your business that you're likely to get asked over, and over again.

You can use 1 Layer Deep™ to map out all the processes in your business and get every single question answered, documented, and stored. And I'm going to show you how to do that, so your team can be ready in any event, even an emergency. But in this chapter, we're going to start with quick wins.

If I told you I can gain you ten hours a week with one hour of time right now, would you say, "yes!" or "h\Hell yes!"? That's what we're going to do in this hyper quick chapter— I'm going to show you how to eliminate the most common questions and problems in your business, and after you'll be hooked. Like a good piece of bacon, you'll just want more.

SOPs vs Microplays

When I first started in business, I struggled for years to figure out how to make my companies run more efficiently. Eventually, I dove into the creation of standard operating procedures (SOPs): I opened up a Google Doc, titled one of them "Finance," and started writing down every single detail of every single task within Finance. *If I have all the related information in one place, everyone will know where to find it, right?* Well. . . my team read about 0 percent of what I wrote.

The modern attention span is far too short to consume 5,000 words on, "This is how you run the finance department." Instead, when an employee wants to know the policy on something money-related, they're probably thinking more specifically about an immediate problem: *When is it appropriate to charge our clients a late fee?*

Because that's how people are increasingly consuming information. They don't consume information via long-winded, overwrought, complex novels that deal with every task within a department. These sorts of standard operating procedures sit on a server and gather virtual dust. We need to think more like an influencer posting on TikTok. When a social media guru posts something, they would think: *What's a highly specific question I can answer for my audience in under two minutes?*

They start there, because that's what audiences are looking for: TikTok users will scroll to pick up hidden tips on how to catch a girl's attention, how to be a better mom, how to negotiate a salary increase at a large company, etc. Today's audiences want the specific solution to solve the specific problem they are facing *right now*. And that's the sort of information your employees will *use*. So, after creating beautiful standard operating procedures no one read or used, I started thinking more like a TikTok creator, and I came up with Microplays: Two-minute, one-step answers.

And guess what? Now my employees *love* our employee portal, and they actually use the information.

Microplay: The 2-minute 1-step answer.

I don't use standard operating procedures because that idea comes pre-loaded and quite simply, most standard operating procedures aren't made for employees. They're long, boring, and created before technology really took off. Microplays, on the other hand, suggest highly targeted information that can be read in under two minutes. Take a look at how Microplays come out against typical standard operating procedures:

Traditional SOP's VS Microplays		
Length →	10-30 pages	Under 250 words
Application →	Covers everything (too much)	Targets one real task or situation
Tone →	Formal, corporate outdated	Conversational, clear, specific
Flexibility →	Rigid	Modular, adaptable
Use rate →	Rarely read, often ignored	Designed to be used daily
Outcome →	"Write it once" and hope	"Use it now" to solve and scale

Why Microplays Work

- **People don't read standard operating procedures,** but they *will* follow a two-minute instruction that makes their job easier.
- **It removes the owner as the bottleneck,** no more being the help desk.
- **It creates a scalable business** that doesn't rely on your memory, energy, or inbox.
- **It fits today's team habits,** quick answers, on-the-go access, just-in-time learning.

- **It's ego-breaking and empowering,** because letting go doesn't mean giving up control; it means distributing it smartly.

"BLANK, AND"

When employees are struggling with a problem, and they want a solution, there's a pattern that often emerges to the way they're asking a question. Again, they *don't* think, *I should click the Finance folder, then Customers, then Late customers, Then Templates,* and so on. More likely, they'll think *I'm sending out an invoice for the third time AND I want to know what to say.* Or, *I'm going to be late to work AND I need to call someone.* Or, *I'm running a new marketing campaign AND I want to know my budget.*

Notice the pattern? It's *blank* situation, AND I need *blank* information. I've shortened this pattern even further and I call it "BLANK, AND." No, not *all* Microplays are in this format. A Microplay is simply an instruction that is crystal clear, handles one specific task, and is under two minutes. *But* the BLANK, AND is the quickest, most efficient way of building out your first Microplays. In the next chapter, we'll discuss how to build Microplays that are not so straightforward.

The BLANK, AND pattern works well not only because it's how people *think* but because it's also how people often *search* for information, so you can literally use their questions as the answers to the titles of your documents. Imagine if your top questions were laid out in documents entitled the following:

- "I'm running late AND I want to know what to do?"
- "We ran out of a product AND I want to know how to reorder it quickly."
- "I'm trying to login AND I forgot my credentials."

Then, in each of those documents, you have information in two-minute snippets on how to solve *that exact problem.* I can tell you from experience: your employees will use those! I bet you can think of thirty questions, right now, that would save you massive time if they were answered. But you don't need thirty—you only need ten.

How to Create Your First Ten Microplays

Here's how to create your first Microplays, ten miniature documents that will save you hours and hours every week:

1: Set a timer for sixty minutes

2: Build your questions list

- Get out a pen and paper and just start physically writing down the questions that *you know* someone is going to ask you in the next twenty-four business hours.
- Then, continue building your list: Ask your top managers (if you have them) what questions they're being asked over, and over again.

- Or review your recent messages (Slack, email, WhatsApp) for the questions that keep coming up. You can also export those threads and run them through AI to quickly spot the top recurring ones.

3: Simplify to "BLANK, AND"

Simplify and rewrite everything in the "BLANK, AND" pattern from the *employee's perspective*. Here's how this may look:

> "I'm late to work AND I'm going to miss my shift."

> "I need this software AND I don't know how much money I can spend."

> "I ran out of __ AND I need to order more of it."

4: Edit down to ten

You're probably going to come up with more than ten questions, and that's good. It means you're digging deep and pulling out the real issues. But don't try to solve them all at once. Cut the list down to ten. This keeps the process simple and keeps you from getting overwhelmed. The goal isn't to fix every problem in your business right away. The goal is to build the habit of documenting answers in a clear, usable way.

Ten is enough to move the needle. It forces you to pick the most common, time-sucking questions and put your energy where it will make the biggest difference. That creates quick wins you and your team can actually feel, and builds momentum without burning you out or overcomplicating things. Think of it as training your "documentation muscle" before you move on to heavier work.

5: Create the docs

Once you have the list down to ten, create ten different docs (or ten tabs within a doc), using the BLANK, AND statement (or question) as the *actual titles* of those documents. Don't worry about uploading them to a portal or overthinking where they'll live yet. The goal here is just to practice writing Microplays. Keep it simple. (1 Layer Deep™)

6: Document the Microplay

Click on each document and fill in the answers. Put in any links, passwords, or screenshots you can create in a minute or two. Don't worry about making this perfect. Just get the information. Down

7: Stop the timer

Congratulations: You just saved yourself ten hours this week, and every other week, by never having to answer those questions again.

When you're finished, your documents should look like this:

Name
☐ 1: A customer hasn't paid AND how do I get them to pay?
☐ 2: A customer is requesting a refund AND I don't know when/if we offer those?
☐ 3: A customer wants to tip us AND I don't know if we're allowed to take them?
☐ 4: I'm at a clients house AND I spilled something on their carpet?
☐ 5: I'm going to be late to a clients house AND I want to know how to proceed

Tips on Creating Your First Ten Microplays

Here's a few tips on crushing this:

Ignore Grammar Rules

Go back to the example. Notice that the grammar is Libby-style: Like an eighth grader wrote it. The point is to frontload the important information *before* the "AND," so the title is eye-catching. So, be willing to cut corners grammatically to get the words or phrases such as "customer" "weather" or "ran out" as the first few words early-on. Further, don't worry that some of the titles are questions that end in question marks and some are statements that end in periods. It doesn't matter; just write what feels most natural.

Put a Number Before the Title

If you put a number before any words, most alphabetical filing systems will then file these documents numerically first, before any others. So, label each one with a number, then the title, like this. This will ensure that these ten Microplays stay at the top of your portal or drive.

Write From Their Perspective

Ensure that the title is written from the employee's perspective. So, *"I'm* running late to work," not *"You're* running late to work."

Write for Stability

You must be willing to pick one path to solve one problem and move forward. (You can edit/change it later). One of the benefits of documenting your Microplays is the forcing function that will result—you, the owner, will be forced to decide how you want something done. If you've been telling five different people five different ways to solve the same problem, of course no one's been doing it the "right way." There *is* no right way. Just pick one path: If you want employees to *never* refund customers, write that. If you want them to refund customers every time if it's less than $50, write that. You can change your Microplay anytime you want. Standardization leads to implementation which leads to iteration.

Ensure It Can Be Read in < Two Minutes

Make sure your Microplay can be read in less than two minutes. If your entire Microplay takes the average person longer than two minutes to read, no one will.

Don't Use AI in the First Round

One benefit of creating these Microplays is that you'll gain quick insights into your company. You may realize that you don't have a process at all, that a cheap piece of software could solve a major gap, or that one of your employees has come up with a smarter way of doing something you actually like better. But you won't get those benefits if you outsource the thinking to AI.

When you let AI do the heavy lifting, you skip the part of the process that makes it stick. Writing in your own words forces you to slow down, process what's really happening, and make decisions in your language. That act of recall, pulling it out of your head and putting it on paper, is what wires the knowledge into your brain. It's the difference between hearing something once and actually remembering it when you need to implement.

There's also a spatial element to it. Your brain remembers where you wrote things, the words you chose, the order you put them in. That spatial recognition gives you a mental map of your own process. If you hand it all over to AI, you lose that map, and with it, your ability to remember or act on what you learned.

And here's the issue: if you let AI write it for you and it breaks, you won't know how to fix it. You won't even understand it, because it was never written in your language in the first place.

So do this work yourself first. Get your messy thoughts down, even if it's not perfect. Then, once you've captured it in your own voice, that's the time to use AI to clean it up for grammar, proofreading, or condensing. But the thinking, the clarity, and the breakthroughs have to come from you.

Progress over Perfection

With your first Microplays, the goal isn't a perfection solution that works every time. Honestly, you're shooting for about an 80 percent success rate here. Let's do some math:

Let's say that 50 percent of the questions you're getting answered every day are one of the ten questions you've answered inside these Microplays. Then, let's say that 80 percent of the time, an employee will actually use the Microplay to solve that problem. That's a total success rate of 40 percent of all questions being answered,[11] *without* your involvement. Assuming you're losing two and a half hours a day answering those questions over email, Slack, quick meetings, text messages, etc., you'll be saving one hour a day. But that's not it: You've also *standardized* the process to solving those problems the way you want them solved. Think of all the repeatable tasks that are currently getting done incorrectly, that are causing you (and your team) to redo them? If you're anything like most business owners, standardizing frequent solutions to frequent scenarios will save you *at a minimum* of one hour a day in efficiency and not having to re-do work. So that's now two hours a day, or ten hours a week, every week!

---

[11] 50% X 80% = 40%

Leave it in Draft

Don't feel like you must finish a Microplay the first time you write it. You can always leave it in draft. Some Microplays need to be tested, run, and adjusted before they're solid. When you leave it in draft, you take the pressure off yourself. You capture the idea, move on, and come back later to tweak it. A simple way to mark this is by adding [Draft] to the title, so everyone knows it's still a work in progress. That's how most good Microplays are built—step by step, not all at once.

The goal isn't perfect. The goal is progress: a draft gets you moving, and moving is what makes the system work.

Put a Time Limit on This

Give yourself one hour to create all ten of these Microplays. That's an average of six minutes per question. This time limit will do two things:

1) It will ensure that you aren't over-complicating the answers.
2) With only an hour, *you* won't feel overwhelmed. Most business owners don't create standardized processes because they think it's too time-consuming. So, give yourself an hour, and watch that one hour pay back ten times the investment within a week.

***

While these ten Microplays may give you massive relief in knowing that you won't have to answer those questions again, it will also give your employees massive relief! While you're trying to save time and be more efficient, your employees want stability. This will make them breathe easier.

Pro Tip: There is No Right Way

If you've been telling five different people five different ways to solve the same problem, of course no one's been doing it the "right way." There *is* no right way.

Just Steal Them. I'm Giving You Permission

I'll bet that you can come up with the top ten questions that are driving you crazy, right now. But you don't have to. I've done it for you. You can go online to 1layerdeep.com/resources, where I have a growing list of Microplays by industry, customer, problem, etc. And you can find your business, or a very close analog, then just copy and paste those Microplays for free, or you can browse and steal ideas.

Or, if you don't want to go online, I've written out the ten most helpful questions, that, when solved, save nearly any business massive time. You can copy and paste these into ten new documents, then, inside the documents, write down how you want this issue to be solved at your company:

Ten Microplays Every Business Should Have

1. A customer hasn't paid AND how do I get them to pay?

2. A customer is requesting a refund AND I don't know when/if we offer those?

3. A customer wants to give us a tip AND I don't know if we're allowed to take them?

4. I'm at a client's house AND I spilled something on their carpet?

5. I'm going to be late to a client's house AND I want to know how to proceed

6. I'm trying to get into a customer's home AND the code isn't working

7. There's a dog AND it's barking

8. We ran out of a product AND how do I/should I order more?

9. There's a weather warning AND I don't know if we continue working in this weather?

10. A customer wants to pay for another service AND I'm not a salesperson

Ten Hours+

Remember that Microplays are tools to make your company more efficient and autonomous; as long as they're doing that, they're working. Microplays embody the 1 Layer Deep™ ethos to remove the dependency from any one person: the shortest path to get to the result

While this 1 Layer Deep™ trick will save you ten hours this week, over time, the effects will compound. Employees will see how easy they are to use, and they'll be hooked. *You'll* get hooked on delivering standardized processes in microformat. Everyone will see how easy it is to create and use Microplays.

And if you're thinking, *Hey, didn't you say that not ALL Microplays are in the BLANK, AND format?* Yes, yes I did.

And we'll get to those in the next chapter!

CHAPTER 4

The "Right" Framework for Microplays

In the last chapter, we focused on how to think about Microplays in a fast, down-and-dirty way, mainly around titling and building your first set so you could win back ten hours by eliminating those repeated questions. This chapter takes the next step: diving into the actual internal structure of a Microplay.

We talked about the BLANK, AND version of Microplays, which is the easiest way to get going with Microplays.

But here's what I want to say:

Everything you do should be in Microplays.

Need to teach how to run payroll? Do it in a Microplay. A

two-minute instruction, with the login, password, and probably even a screenshot all right there. Need to show someone how to ask a great interview question? Do it in a quick, two-minute instructional (which may just have a forty-five-second video in it).

Some of these questions may not quite fit into BLANK, AND, or at least, that would feel silly: "I'm trying to run payroll AND I need to look up how to run payroll." Honestly, it still works, but truthfully, I use BLANK, AND mostly for the frontline questions I'm tired of answering.

For other areas, I still use Microplays, and they still mean the same basic thing (a two-minute, one-step instruction designed to tackle a specific problem), but I design them a little differently. The most important thing is *not* that they are in BLANK, AND, but rather, that no matter what, they follow CAPT:

> *Context: The right information (to the right person)*
>
> *Action: done the right way*
>
> *Priorities: with the right focus*
>
> *Timeframe: at the right time*

CAPT

Context → Right info 📄 Right person 👤
Action → Done the right way ☑
Priorities → With the right focus 🔍
Timeframe → At the right time 🕐

Let's get into it!

Context: The Right Information (To the Right Person)

The first thing that your Microplay should have is context. A huge problem that the traditional standard operating procedures have is that they are disjointed from the actual situation that our people are in. Or, they're written *to the wrong person.*

Context is about delivering the right information to the right person. If it's written for the wrong audience, or stripped of the situation the employee is actually in, it will fall flat.

I run both a house cleaning business and a software company, among others. These industries have different languages, even when dealing with the same issues. Further, within the same company, my sales teams and my employees in customer service may be dealing with similar issues (such as how to take a credit card payment) but they're probably thinking in different ways about that problem.

By making context one of the first things we talk about, we connect the Microplay to the employee.

For instance, if you were going to create a Microplay for employees to call out of work, the nuances matter: Is it because the employee is sick, because they're running late, or they just need a day off? The context is one pillar of Microplays where it's better to be more detailed than less detailed. You wouldn't want to create a Microplay entitled "How to Talk to a Customer." You'd want one that was more detailed like, "How to deal with an angry customer over email who wants more than $X back." Or, if you were going to put this in BLANK, AND, it could be, "A customer is angry over email AND I want to know what to write."

Actions: Done The Right Way

This brings us to the next pillar of the Microplay. The main idea, the meat and pickles, as I like to say. It can be tempting to make this piece long and drawn out, and explain in length what to do and how to do it. This is what I did when I started out. I thought the more I got into the nitty gritty and explained every detail, the better my team would function. But this isn't helpful for us or our employees. If we keep the Microplay short, sweet, and to the point, our employees are far more likely to read and understand it. Actions are only useful if they're done the right way. The goal of a Microplay isn't to overwhelm. It's to give your team the exact next step so they can execute confidently and correctly.

Remember: two minutes or less. Aside from making it more digestible for our employees, this forces us to decide what's truly important.

The less talked about aspect of this pillar is how useful it is in emergency situations. In mundane, everyday scenarios, we can get by OK without direction. We generally know what we need to get done. In emergencies, though, Microplays are useful for a different reason. Just like the new hires don't have much experience with your company and procedures, in emergency situations, we all lack experience. We all need someone telling us what to do. We can use Microplays, with their hyper specific actions to do this. It's a way of putting our procedures in stone so that in future stressful situations, we can have direction from someone not affected by the heat of the moment. When I was in the path of the hurricane, I felt more pressure than I've ever felt before. I could feel the eyes of all of the people looking to me; in my mind, I could see myself trying to carry all of them and falling. I'm not sure how we would have fared without our Microplays, but because we had them, I didn't have to make the big decisions. We simply followed the workflows. In that moment, I realized the true impact that Microplays could really have. I didn't have to worry about trying to figure out what was most important because it was already in the Microplays.

Priorities: With The Right Focus

Imagine you're a prehistoric human. You're walking along, minding your own business (no pun intended) when a saber-tooth tiger lunges out of the woods and starts heading straight for you. You turn to run, but at that moment, your stomach growls. Seeing a berry bush along the path, you stop to pick some to fill your rumbling belly. And that's when you meet an untimely demise in the jaws of the saber-toothed tiger. This is what you would do *without* priorities. Starting over, but *with* priorities, you would ignore your hunger, run right past the berry bush, and not stop running until your life was no longer in danger. Priorities are about the right focus. Without them, employees can get distracted chasing what feels urgent but isn't truly important. With the right focus built into the Microplay, they'll know exactly what to do first.

In the case of the tiger and the berries, priorities are necessary and clear, but in other cases, they may be necessary, but they aren't necessarily clear, at least not to your employees: Just because it's obvious to you that payroll comes before responding to Facebook comments, doesn't mean it will be just as obvious to your people. Each Microplay should fill in this gap for your employees, if necessary.

Often, a Microplay is obvious in prioritization because it handles such a specific task. But other times, it is not so obvious. For instance, if someone falls and starts bleeding, should you immediately call 911, a manager, etc.? We have a

Microplay that says simply:

Determine how serious the injury is first, then:

- *If dire, call 911 immediately, then call the office immediately after*

or

- *Contact management if immediate help is not required*

In other Microplays, when someone says they're running late, we offer the prioritization (depending on the *context*) on who to call first—the client, or the office.

Timeframe: At The Right Time

Most of us have spent extra time on things we don't need to. We spend an hour checking our email, forty-five minutes making a to-do list, or half an hour on a quick check-in with employees. Our employees do the same things, as much as and sometimes more than we do. This isn't beneficial for them or us. We aren't getting as much productivity as we could be getting, and they get to the end of their day with a feeling of dissatisfaction. The way to combat this is by including a timeframe in our Microplays. If the task at hand is answering emails, give ten minutes for it. If it's something more intensive, like cleaning a house, then decide how much time to give them. Giving the perfect amount of time isn't important because people will usually rise or fall to the amount of time you give them (if the time is within reason). If you give Nancy fifteen minutes to log into her computer, she will probably take fifteen minutes. On the flip side, if you only give her ten minutes to have a check-in meeting, she will be more productive with her time in the meeting. As long as we are in the right ballpark, the exact amount of time is not overly important. It's more about having a specific amount of time that we can be held accountable to. According to a survey in 2023, nearly two-thirds of employees said they wasted two hours a day because of a lack of deadlines. Apparently, even employees know they would be more productive when working within a timeframe.

Timeframes keep people working at the right time. Without a time boundary, tasks stretch endlessly but with a clear timeframe, employees channel their energy where it matters most.

Once, Tom was going to clean a house but didn't get an answer at the door. By the time I found out about the situation, several hours had gone by. When I asked him why he was still at the house, he said it was because he hadn't gotten a call from Nancy and the office. When I asked the office why they hadn't called and told them to move on, Nancy said they hadn't gotten a call back from the customer. This highlights another way that time can be used in Microplays: in the extenuating circumstances. In an ideal world, I would have had a Microplay for what to do if the customer doesn't answer the door. In the Microplay, I would have included the key ingredient of time by telling them how long they should wait before moving on. Because I didn't, they wasted the entire day. That's why every Microplay has to deliver the right information, to the right person, the right way, with the right focus, at the right time. When each of these pieces is in place, the system works, without you hovering over it.

Pro Tip: Always Remember: 1 Layer Deep™

The point of 1 Layer Deep™ is to make success as easy and simple as possible. If Tom gets a flat tire, he needs to call the office. Following the rule 1 Layer Deep™, the phone number should be in the Microplay so that he can call it directly from the page rather than having to search for the number. Or say Nancy got the call from Tom that he got a flat and would need to reschedule. Instead of having to open another window and find the database of customer numbers, the database should be linked at the bottom of the Microplay so she could easily access it directly from the Microplay.

Don't Be Strict about "The Right" Microplay

Context, Actions, Priorities, and Timeframe are necessary elements of a Microplay (the right information for the right person, done the right way, with the right focus, at the right time), but truthfully, not every Microplay needs all of them, or sometimes they're implied. If the Microplay is on "What Is the Office Number?" you shouldn't be going through *CAPT* exactly. Essentially, use these as a framework for when creating a Microplay, but when a simpler answer works, give it!

Putting It All Together

So, how should this look in the end?

The BLANK, AND Microplays are a bit easier to conceptualize—but for the rest of any Microplays, you want to group them around what we call "Gameplans"—which is a group of Microplays centered around a specific outcome, which could be something like "What to do If" scenarios, or you could have a Gameplan of "Onboarding" Microplays, which may have Individual Microplays such as: "How to use our Trello board," or "How to setup your 401(k)," etc.

> **Gameplan: A set of Microplays that create a full outcome.**

And if you're thinking, *But where do I put these?* Or *I'm going to need a bunch of these, and how am I going to store all those so they're still accessible?* Those are great questions. . . for the next chapter.

PS: Microplays for Handbooks

Most employees will never sit down and read a forty-page handbook. What they really want are quick answers: *What's the PTO policy? How does attendance work? What's the dress code?* By breaking the handbook into Microplays, every common question is answered in two minutes or less. No flipping through pages, no waiting on HR, and no confusion.

The CAPT Framework

- **Context**: Traditional handbooks often get ignored because they're long, dense, and buried in PDFs. Employees just want quick, clear instructions.

- **Action**: Convert each major policy into a Microplay, a short, step-by-step guide with a clear title such as *How to Request PTO* or *Dress Code Standards*. Each Microplay should take less than two minutes to read and, when possible, include a screenshot or a short clip to show the process.

- **Priorities**: Begin with the policies employees ask about most often, PTO, attendance, dress code, and breaks. Keep the language simple and employee-friendly, skipping legal jargon. Make the Microplays searchable and easy to share so managers can send a link instead of re-explaining policies.

- **Timeframe**: Each Microplay should take no more than two minutes to absorb. By creating two to three per week, you can build a full library of 25–30 micro-policies within three months.

Example Microplays

How to Request PTO might show a short video of where to log in, a screenshot of the form, and a reminder about the required notice period.

Attendance Policy could be distilled into one sentence, such as: "Clocking in after 8:05 a.m. counts as tardy."

Dress Code / Uniform Reminder might include a simple graphic or photo showing what's acceptable, which can be re-sent seasonally as a refresher.

Break Policy can be summarized in two sentences explaining when and how breaks should be taken.

Positioning Micropolices

Think "micro-policies": quick, clear, and always at your team's fingertips. Instead of hunting through a thick handbook, employees get answers in under two minutes, and managers save time by sharing a link instead of repeating the same explanations.

1 Layer Deep™ Personal Application

Microplays in Your Personal Life

My family was visiting Oklahoma. My husband, my seven-year-old daughter, and my twenty-seven-year-old son; we were all there except my seventeen-year-old son, whom we left behind to watch the house. You may think you know where the story is going: we get tons of calls from him about the things we asked him to do, or the house and animals go uncared for, right? Or even worse, something goes really wrong, and we have to fly back and take care of it for him. But none of this happened. But a big mishap did happen. The water went out while we were gone. The only thing is, we didn't even hear about it until the next time we saw our son. How was our seventeen-year-old able to handle the situation without even needing to call us? Our secret? We have a "family portal" with Microplays for our *household*.

We use Microplays throughout our home for anyone who may need them, from ourselves to our kids to our cleaners to our babysitters and house watchers. We simply took the logical step from using Microplays and Playbooks in our business to using them in our home, where our children ask as many, if not more, questions. A pillar that we have in our companies is "independently self-motivated." We like to talk about this (half-jokingly) in our home as well: we're creating independently self-motivated children.

Some people like to ask things like "Why should I make Microplays if I'm the only one who would ever use it? I already know what to do." To be completely honest, you shouldn't. Unless you want to keep doing it forever. If you ever want to be free from a task, Microplays are the first step. Even if it's just something you're going to delegate to your kids. Even if you don't have a house cleaner yet, but you plan on having one in the future. If you ever plan on buying back your time, as Dan Martell says, you should document your process. If you don't, you'll be behind when you finally hire somebody and have to start figuring out what your process actually looks like.

Remember from a few chapters ago that each Microplay should be created with the consumer in mind. Some Microplays should be very technical, but for others, like my seven-year-old, smaller words are better. For her, the best would be pictures and videos along with simple explanations. I've found that, where the Microplays for my team need to have more text and videos, in my home, videos are much better for getting the point across. It's not so important where you store them (I have a portal, but Google Drive works, too); it's more important how these are formatted.

While many Microplays are designed to teach someone how to perform a specific task, others, particularly our family Microplays, are there to not to teach but to provide a set of guidelines on how we function as a family. For example, our communication Microplay: When creating this Microplay, we got together as a family and decided how we wanted to communicate with each other: what words we should and shouldn't use, what to do in conflict, what things to communicate about, etc. This gave us a way to hold ourselves accountable. When things start getting heated, we can refer back to our communication Microplay.

Another is our identity Microplay. This one serves as a reminder of *who* we are and what we do. It's a north star, something we can use to orient ourselves and navigate through life. Sometimes we're going to mess up. but because we have our identity written down, our family is able to hold us accountable and get us back on track.

Pro Tip: Microphrases

My husband and I use what we call Microphrases at home with our kids. These are short, specific words or phrases that carry a whole set of instructions inside them. Instead of giving a long lecture or checklist, we use a Microphrase and everyone knows exactly what's expected.

Take the phrase "hotel ready." When we tell our kids a room needs to be hotel ready, they don't need us to spell out: "Pick up the clothes, make the bed, clear the trash, wipe down the surfaces." They already know the standard we're talking about. Hotel ready means the room should look like it belongs in a hotel—clean, neat, and ready for guests.

Microphrases work the same way in business. Think of them as verbal shortcuts to your Microplays. Just like a point guard calling out a play on the court, one phrase cues a whole series of actions without wasting time on overexplaining. When everyone on the team shares the same Microphrases, communication becomes faster, clearer, and less frustrating.

For example, instead of saying, "Please make sure this client's file is organized with notes in the CRM, all emails tagged, and the billing updated," you could simply say, "Make it client-ready." If your Microplay defines what "client-ready" means, your team will instantly know the standard without you having to micromanage every step.

***

And of course, even with my family, everything is 1 Layer Deep™. Even in our family Microplays, I try to make it as easy as possible to do what needs to be done. For instance, in our family portal, there are Gameplans so you can find relevant Microplays based on your context, but there is also a simple search bar. For people trying to get something done around the house, this is the simplest way for them to access whatever resources they need.

The same applies to our short-term rental property; whenever there is a consistent question being asked, we print and frame a QR code to link directly to a Microplay or tool so guests can get the answer instantly. The biggest one by far that's saved us time is Wi-Fi. I've answered questions from rentals a million times at all hours of the night. Because our vacation cabin sits on the highest peak on the Georgia mountains, there's no cell signal, so guests can't dig through their emails to pull up our welcome message with directions on how to access the home (for some reason, they never look at the welcome message before they arrive). So, what did we do? Printed and framed a QR code right outside the door. Renters can scan it and connect instantly to the Wi-Fi. Problem solved. We've done the same thing now for little things around the cabin as well, hanging framed QR codes for things like blender instructions, turning the shower knobs for hot vs cold water, and operating the gas log fireplace (a big hit in Georgia!). Anything to make the stay easier.

Trying to keep things 1 Layer Deep™ in the home is just as important as keeping them 1 Layer Deep™ in your business. In the modern day, kids are used to things being accessible. Keeping the 1 Layer Deep™ theme in mind when making your portal is what keeps kids engaged with your Microplays. And of course, now, when your kids have a question, you can say, "Hey, that's a really good question. Why don't you check the portal?" If you stick with it and direct them to the family portal, it will catch on. And if you don't have a portal set up yet for your family or your business, you can get started at 1LD.com.

**

The amazing thing about having Microplays in your home is that it clears the smoke. The ambiguity is gone; everyone is clear on what should and shouldn't be done. This goes from house rules like no swearing, no running in the house, or what time to be home, all the way to how often the dog gets taken out and how much he gets fed. All this is super helpful for teaching people (guests or house sitters) who aren't familiar with the rules or chores or how to do them.

Case in point: We signed my seventeen-year-old son up for a basketball camp that was near us while we were in Georgia. That would have left the house alone for the entire month, except my son had a friend who could watch it while we were gone. The crazy thing? We didn't have to teach him anything; everything he needed to know was in the portal already. He took care of the house plants, the yard, the dogs; everything that needed to get done around the house, he was able to do thanks to the Microplays. There weren't any emergencies, but if there had been, he would have been able to deal with them just like my son did when the water went out.

The final thing I'll leave you with is this. Imagine you're in a meeting, on an airplane, or preoccupied some other way. Then you get a call. It's from your kid; they have another question about something around the house. Now you're going to have to mute yourself in the meeting and answer the phone, and try and remember the answer to whatever question they have. But what if you didn't have to? What if all you had to do was text them: check the portal.

CHAPTER 5

From Microplays to Gameplans (& Beyond)

Have you used the Microplays yet? Did they change your life?

If you used them at all, you were probably thinking, *This works great, for about ten Microplays. How can I possibly scale beyond that?*

In this chapter, you're going to see how to turbocharge your entire business and put dozens of Microplays into practice. But first, we need to get everything out on the table. (And I mean *everything*.)

***

Do you ever have those days where you just decide: it's finally time, I'm going to clean out my closet? You roll up your sleeves and bury your arms up to the elbow in piles of clothes, sorting and folding and turning your room into a disaster area for the sake of consolidating and pruning your outfits. This is the time when you find all of the clothes that don't belong or no longer serve a purpose. The seven pairs of black jeans, the turtlenecks that you never wear, the shirts you saved for painting in and never used. All the extra clothing you thought you needed but don't. Not only do you find extra things, but you also find a lack of things that you do need. Suddenly, you realize you only have long-sleeved shirts, you don't have a single belt that you like wearing, and the last time your shorts were in style was two decades ago. You realize it was a good thing that you went through your wardrobe; in some places, it was spread way too thin, and in others, there was a lot of excess.

That's what we're going to do in *this* chapter. We're going to get everything out on the table; we're going to take apart your business, then put it back together in one chapter, and in doing so, we'll create Microplays, Gameplans, and Owner Playbooks (we'll get into all these soon).

Zoom out:

Gameplans	=	management-level	**strategy**.
Microplays	=	operational-level	**tactics**.

Traditional playbooks try to do everything and end up helping no one **in the moment**—that's why we don't use them.

This can feel like a lot. That's why I try to give people a quick win with their first ten Microplays, so they don't feel overwhelmed when it's time to "clean out the closet." For all my tech founders, it's the MVP (minimum viable product) that gets your foot in the door. It's like that in most areas of life:

- Before you start running a marathon, just go for a walk.
- Before you decide to change your entire diet, try a smoothie.
- Before you start a company, try doing one freelance job.

A quick win will give you the necessary energy that will spark a new belief: *If I feel this good with 1 percent effort, how would I feel if I dove in headfirst?*

The other benefit of starting with Microplays is this:

They're the foundation for organizing your entire business.

My 1 Layer Deep™ method has different versions you can apply based on your situation, but the foundation for business owners is always the same: What's the one action you need to get to the result you want? That's what the Microplays provide.

But of course, you can't have 1oo million Microplays all listed out and numbered o -1oo,ooo,ooo. So, here's the full system:

- **Roles: Someone's position in your "business field."** *(Think manager or technician.)*
- **Microplay: The 2-minute 1-step answer.** *(You know these!)*
- **Gameplan: A set of Microplays that create a full outcome.** *(An "Onboarding Gameplan" or an "Emergency Gameplan," or a "Payroll Gameplan.")*
- **Owner Playbook: The master libraries of Microplays & Gameplans.** *(Most companies have two Owner Playbooks, one for front-of-house and one for back-of-house processes.)*

So, Microplays are the short quick answers to specific problems. Then, when you bundle a group of these together that are all related, we call that a Gameplan. The Owner Playbook is the repository of all Microplays and Gameplans; I've found it useful to have *two* of these: One for front-of-house (front-line employees), and one for back-of-house (office staff), though some businesses may only need one.

Here's a visual representation:

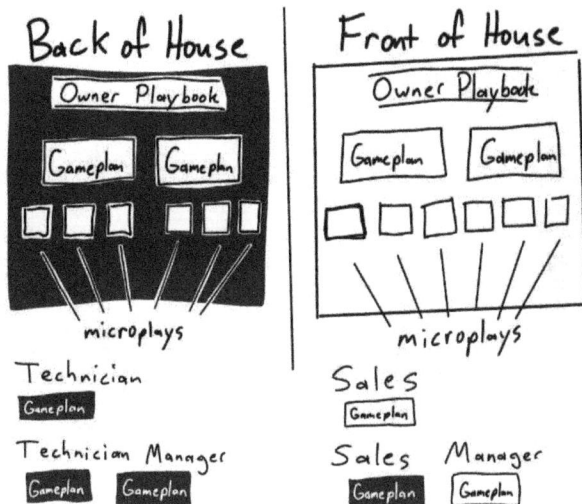

I hope you like pictures, because this chapter's going to have a lot of them. (If you're listening on audio, plug in that good ol' imagination!)

***

A lot of people ask me how this actually looks and actually works. I'm not a huge fan of Google Drive, but let's be honest. . . that's probably what you're going to use to get started, so learn to love it. I've put a "WHAT IF" Gameplan for Technicians together below:

Owner's Playbook for Technicians			
Status	Category	MicroPlays	Date Updated
	Video	I need to contact the office AND...	
GOOD TO GO ▾	☐	～～～～	2025 ▾
GOOD TO GO ▾	☐	～～ ～～～～ ～～	2023 ▾
GOOD TO GO ▾	☐	～～～～～	2025 ▾
GOOD TO GO ▾	☐	～～ ～～～～	2025 ▾
GOOD TO GO ▾	☐	～～～ ～～～ ～～～	2025 ▾
GOOD TO GO ▾	☐	～～ ～～ ～～	2025 ▾
		I'm driving AND...	
GOOD TO GO ▾	☐	～～～ ～～～～	2025 ▾
GOOD TO GO ▾	☐	～～～	2025 ▾
		I arrive at a home AND...	
GOOD TO GO ▾	☐	～～～	2024 ▾
GOOD TO GO ▾	☑	～～～ ～～	2024 ▾
GOOD TO GO ▾	☐	～～～～～～	2024 ▾
GOOD TO GO ▾	☑	～～～～	2024 ▾
GOOD TO GO ▾	☐	～～～～	2024 ▾
		I'm entering a home AND...	
GOOD TO GO ▾	☐	～～～～～	2024 ▾
GOOD TO GO ▾	☑	～～～	2024 ▾
GOOD TO GO ▾	☐	～～～～～～～	2024 ▾
GOOD TO GO ▾	☐	～～～～～	2024 ▾
GOOD TO GO ▾	☐	～～ ～～～	2024 ▾
		I'm cleaning AND...	

| Gameplan: What ▾ | Gameplan: Onboarding ▾ | Gameplan: Company Policies ▾ | G |

You can add additional columns as you go along if they're helpful and necessary, always remembering to keep with the 1 Layer Deep™ method: *one* action to get what you need. You already know how to create a few Microplays. Now, let's go deeper and organize your entire company.

Hiring ≠ Delegation

To start, we're going to map how your company currently runs, so we can find where the holes are. The problem right now is, you may have delegated stuff, but it's not getting done the way you want it to be done. The cold, hard reality is:

If you're constantly having to go back and check the work of people you've hired, you're not buying back your time; you're buying back inefficiencies. The way to get true relief, the only way to get peace of mind, is to transfer ownership of the outcome. What I mean by that is when you hire people, you're hiring them not only to perform an action but to produce an outcome. At the simplest level, I can hire somebody to push a broom, or I can hire them to clean a floor.

And that's the purpose of *Roles*. Roles are how you make sure the **right people** are assigned to the **right outcomes**. Inside the Owner Playbook, that means you can look at your library of Gameplans and "assign" them to the Role responsible. So, once we map out the "Sales Follow up Gameplan" for example, you can assign that Gameplan to an individual or individuals, and now, they know that Sales follow-up is their job. And to execute, once you've created the Microplays, they simply run them within that Gameplan.

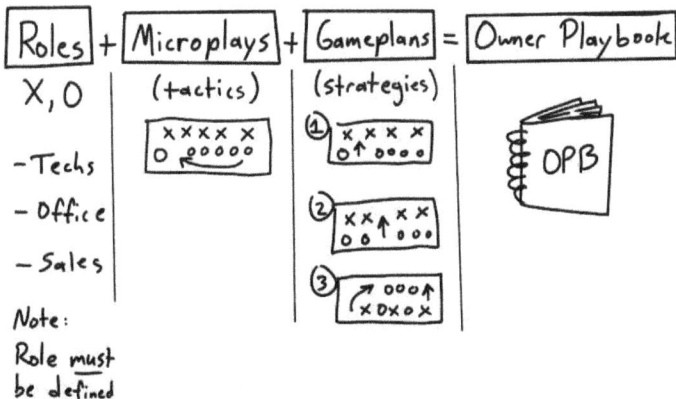

So, that's where we start, with role mapping. From there, we simplify outcomes to 1 Layer Deep™, then, we fix the fire that's worst, and we start attacking. Hopefully, this reminds you of the pattern we discussed earlier: Align, Delete, Execute.

1)   Role Mapping (Align on the Roles and associated Gameplans)

2)   Simplify outcomes to 1 Layer Deep™. (Delete unnecessary friction)

3)   Fix the Fire (Execute on what's most important)

⇉ **Align**
✕ **Delete**
◎ **Execute**

1: Role Mapping

The first step is to map your company but not the way you've been told to do it before. We're not building a traditional Org Chart. Org Charts are about hierarchy: who reports to who, whose name sits in which box. That's not what this is.

What we're doing is building a play map. Think of it like basketball. An Org Chart is about where the players sit on the bench. A play map is about how the ball moves down the court to score points. We care less about who reports to who and more about how the work actually gets done, and how to get "Michael Jordan" the ball so he can sink it every time.

This is why our approach looks so different from EOS or other business frameworks. We're not trying to design the perfect tree of seats and reporting lines. We're designing a system that makes execution faster, clearer, and more reliable.

The easiest way to do this? Grab a few sticky notes (yes, I know—I'm not a fan either). But trust me, they work. Use three or more colors if you can, and a pen.

Roles

When I say, "write down every role in your company," I don't mean names or titles. Not "Emily," but "Sales." Not "Trish," but "Payroll." Roles are the building blocks of your business—the things that must get done, regardless of who does them.

Lay them all out in front of you. Sticky notes on a wall, notecards on a table, whatever works. Make the invisible visible. This is where things get real.

And don't forget to include the roles you're carrying yourself. "Onboarding," "Customer Satisfaction," "Finances"—you'll quickly see why you're burned out. You're trying to play every position on the court at once.

Here's the key: one person can hold more than one role. Just like a basketball player switches from offense to defense depending on which side of the court they're on, you might be in a "sales" role during a discovery call, then switch to "finance" later that afternoon when you're reconciling invoices. Different role, same player.

By mapping out roles instead of people, you start to see:

- Where the gaps are.
- Where you're overextending yourself.
- Where you need to add players.

This clarity is what sets the stage for Gameplans and Microplays later on.

Why This Isn't an Org Chart

Org Charts show seats and hierarchy. Our mapping shows flow and function.

Traditional Org Charts look like a family tree: the owner at the top, managers below, staff below them. That works if all you care about is reporting lines. But when it comes to execution, Org Charts are clunky. They don't tell you how to actually get the ball to the player who can score.

Our system is closer to a swim lanes map. Each lane represents a role. Tasks and actions move across lanes like plays in motion. It's about clarity of responsibility and flow of work, not about rank or seniority.

From Roles to Plays

This is why we do the exercise this way. Once you've laid out all the roles and tasks, you can start grouping them, tossing out redundancies, and streamlining. Instead of a static chart that hangs on the wall, you've now got a dynamic playbook

And this is where it gets fun. With the raw material of roles and tasks in front of you, you can start to design Gameplans (outcomes) and then break them down into Microplays (specific two-minute instructions).

Org Charts keep you stuck in hierarchy. Role mapping sets you up for execution. That's the difference—and it's the reason this approach works.

When you're finished, it should look something like this:

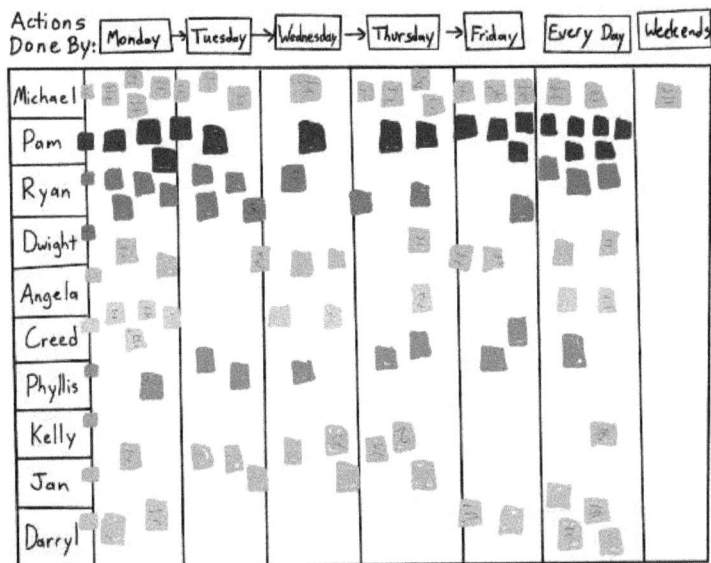

2: Simplify Outcomes (Delete)

Once you've mapped your roles and tasks, the next step is to simplify. If what you've written down looks like a wall of sticky notes that only makes sense to you, then you've missed the point.

In their book *Rework* (and frequently in their insightful talks and blog posts), Jason Fried and David Heinemeier Hansson of Basecamp share a straightforward yet powerful idea: if your process or strategic plan can't fit neatly onto the back of a bar napkin, it's probably too complicated.[12]

This "bar napkin" mentality perfectly aligns with the central message of 1 Layer Deep™: cutting through surface-level complexity to zero-in on what genuinely matters. Or, as we like to simplify: Cut the bullshit and get what you want (or what your business needs). This principle isn't just about simplicity—it's about alignment, deletion, and execution. By keeping things simple and clear, Basecamp has managed to succeed in an industry often overwhelmed by burnout and needless complication.

Incorporating this insight into 1 Layer Deep™ serves as a clear and powerful reminder: the real magic doesn't come from intricate methods or overly detailed procedures. Instead, success comes from simplicity, clarity, and taking

---

[12] Jason Fried and David Heinemeier Hansson, *Rework* (London: Vermilion, 2020).

focused, purposeful action.

So, go back to your wall of roles and tasks:

- Where can you collapse two sticky notes into one?
- Where are you duplicating effort?
- Are there roles with no accountability?
- Are there tasks that exist only because someone created busy work?

Your job here is to strip it down until what's left is so clear that anyone can walk up, glance at it, and know how the work flows. Think "Gameplan chalkboard," not "corporate org binder."

3: Fix the Fire (Execute)

Once you've mapped roles and simplified outcomes, the next step is execution: fixing what's most broken. Think of this like building an ROI Roadmap. The question isn't just, where is the fire? The real question is, which fire, if put out, gives us the biggest return in time, money, or sanity?

Every business has fires. Some are small and annoying; others are major and costly. You can't fix them all at once. But if you focus on the fire that delivers the highest ROI when fixed, you create breathing room for everything else to improve.

Here are the three levels where fires usually show up:

- Frontline: the people in direct contact with customers or delivering the product.
- Management: the people overseeing the frontline.
- Strategic Leadership: the people steering the ship (sometimes that's just you).

The key is prioritization. Which fire, if fixed, creates the most leverage? Which one frees up the most money, saves the most time, or clears the biggest bottleneck?

When I ran this process at my cleaning company in 2019, the biggest ROI was fixing the frontline. My cleaners were overwhelmed and making costly mistakes. By streamlining their systems with Microplays, we freed up hours of wasted time and reduced turnover, which gave management (and me) space to breathe.

At my software company, the ROI was different. The frontline wasn't the issue. Leadership was. Fixing the fire there meant realigning key leaders and redistributing responsibilities. That's what gave us the highest return, because without fixing leadership first, every other problem kept resurfacing.

And here's the blunt truth: nine times out of ten, the fire isn't the task. It's the person. The wrong person in a role will create endless fires no matter how many Microplays you write. The highest ROI often comes from realigning, repositioning, or replacing the person responsible, not tweaking the checklist.

So, when you're looking at your company map, don't just spot the flames. Build your ROI Roadmap. Fix the fire that gives you the biggest payoff first, and the rest of the business will get easier to run.

From Gameplans to the Owner Playbook

Once you know the areas that need the most work, you just need to create the Microplays and the Gameplans.

Again, Google Drive isn't my favorite, but it's workable as a first step, so, what I've done, as I showed earlier, is use Google Docs for the individuals Microplays, and Google Sheets as a Gameplan with all the related Microplays visible on one screen, so that entire Gameplan really is 1 Layer Deep™. Then, I start a new tab at the bottom and do the same thing with the next Gameplan and so on. That's an Owner Playbook. So basically, one Microplay per doc, one Gameplan per tab. (Want a template you can copy and use right away? Grab it at 1layerdeep.com/resources.)

In the end, it looks like this (I know. *Another* Picture!)

Owner's Playbook for Technicians			
Status	Category	MicroPlays	Date Updated
	Video	I need to contact the office AND ..	
Good To Go ▾	☐	～～～～～	2025 ▾
Good To Go ▾	☐	～～ ～～～ ～～	2025 ▾
Good To Go ▾	☐	～～～～	2025 ▾
Good To Go ▾	☐	～～ ～～～～	2025 ▾
Good To Go ▾	☐	～～ ～～～ ～～～	2025 ▾
Good To Go ▾	☐	～～ ～～	2025 ▾
		I'm driving AND	
Good To Go ▾	☐	～～ ～～～～	2025 ▾
Good To Go ▾	☐	～～	2025 ▾
		I arrive at a home AND...	
Good To Go ▾	☐	～～～	2024 ▾
Good To Go ▾	☑	～～～ ～～	2024 ▾
Good To Go ▾	☐	～～～～～～～	2024 ▾
Good To Go ▾	☑	～～～	2024 ▾
Good To Go ▾	☐	～～～～～	2024 ▾
		I'm entering a home AND...	
Good To Go ▾	☐	～～～～～	2024 ▾
Good To Go ▾	☑	～～～～	2024 ▾
Good To Go ▾	☐	～～～～～	2024 ▾
Good To Go ▾	☐	～～～～～	2024 ▾
Good To Go ▾	☐	～～ ～～～	2024 ▾
		I'm cleaning AND...	

| Gameplan: What ▾ | Gameplan: Onboarding ▾ | Gameplan: Company Policies ▾ | Ga |

Starting with G-Drive

You can also start building your Owner Playbook by beginning with the Gameplans, which is easier for some people to visualize. Say you have a café, and you've determined that the place you want to start fighting the fire is with your front-line café staff. (A great place to start out.) Here's something I might do:

I'd go online to Google Drive and create a New Google Sheet.[13] I'd name that whole file "Front of House Playbook." Then, at the bottom, I might label a tab "What If." Then, I'd

---

[13] Ok, I'd *never* use Google Sheets to start with. I really dislike their platform for this purpose! I'd use my own platform, Organize It!, but if you don't want to use that, then start with Google Sheets!

start at the top and, cell by cell, I'd jot down all the problems (probably in the "BLANK, AND" format): "I'm taking payment AND it's not working." "I'm going to be late to work AND I don't know who to call." "I ran out of an ingredient AND I'm not a manager." I'd list these out in one column. I'd continue to list every micro-problem I could think of; I wouldn't worry about writing down the steps just yet, but I'd write down the BLANK, AND statement or question.

Then, once I was done, I'd have a nice list of all the micro-problems that need Microplays to be micro-solved inside of that one Gameplan, something like this:

- I need to contact the office AND. . . When should I call the office immediately?
- I'm driving AND. . . Can't route the address for directions.
- I arrived at a home AND. . . A pet ran out of the home.
- I'm entering a home AND. . . I'm late for my next house?
- I'm cleaning AND. . . I'm late for my next house?

Then, I'd go create those Microplays, *using the exact titles* as the actual titles of the Microplays and drop the links back in.

The Microplays 2.0 Hack:

If you decided to work on Microplays first (a great suggestion for solving frontline employee problems), then here's a hack:

For every "BLANK, AND" scenario, there are about five to ten *more* related scenarios around which you could create more Microplays. For instance:

I'm taking payment AND. . .

> . . . the credit card machine is down.

> ... the customer doesn't have enough money.

> ... the customer wants me to break a hundred-dollar bill.

> ... the customer wants to tip in cash

> . . . we don't have enough change.

> ... the customer wants to pay by check.

> ... the customer wants to pay for someone else's drinks.

> ... they want me to hold onto their card to pay for their whole company's drinks.

> ... their card gets declined.

> ... the bill they want to pay with is fake.

Guess what? Each one of these represents another Microplay to be made. That's why the BLANK, AND system is so powerful. . . you start out with a particular scenario, and you can then group all *related* scenarios around it, each with their own Microplay that can be read, generally, in under 2 minutes.

Pro Tip: The 2-Minute Rule

Want to catapult your documentation process into action? Try this one-week experiment:

For the next seven days, any time someone asks you a question, don't just answer it. Instead:

- Take under two minutes to write down the answer.
- Deliver that written answer back to the person as a microplay.
- That's it! With every question, you're doing three things at once:
- Solving the immediate problem by giving the answer.
- Capturing the solution so it's reusable in the future.
- Jump-starting your playbook library with real, practical microplays.

In just one week, you'll see how fast your documentation starts building itself—and how much smoother your team runs.

Assigning Roles & Gameplans

Once you've identified the fire and created the Gameplans with their Microplays, the last step is to assign ownership. This isn't about rewriting an Org Chart—you already did the hard work of mapping roles and simplifying. Now it's about making sure the right person owns the right play.

When you hand someone a Gameplan, you're not just saying, "Here are your tasks." You're saying, "Here's the outcome you're responsible for, and here's the exact set of plays to make it happen."

This is where a lot of companies get tripped up. Owners assume it's obvious who owns what—"Of course Tim handles cleaning"—but Tim may not see it that way. Or Ashley thinks she's just managing people, but the payroll responsibilities tied to her role were never spelled out. When you finally hand her the Payroll Gameplan, she laughs and says, "So that's why you've been asking me about it!"

Oftentimes, owners don't realize that the company isn't even aligned on who's responsible for what, so, ultimately, even if someone was hired for a task, no one was in charge of an outcome.

By starting with Align (roles), moving through Delete (simplify), and ending with Execute (fix the fire), you've created a system where Gameplans and Microplays lock into place. The right roles are mapped, the waste is cut, and now every outcome has an owner.

That's not an Org Chart. That's execution clarity.

Let's Recap

Ok, so I know that was an intense chapter, so let's recap. The 1 Layer Deep™ method for business includes the following:

- **Roles: Someone's position in your business.** (Think manager, technician, or even owner.)
- **Microplay: The 2-minute, 1-step answer.** (Think operational-level tactics.)
- **Gameplan: A set of Microplays that create a full outcome.** (Think management-level **strategy** "Onboarding Gameplan," "Emergency Gameplan," or "Payroll Gameplan.")
- **Owner Playbook: The master library of Microplays & Gameplans.** (Most companies have two: one for front-end and one for back-end processes.)

To make headway in your business, you start by:

1. Align: Map your company. Get everything out on the table: every role, every task, every workflow.
2. Delete: Simplify outcomes. Group things together, cut redundancies, and streamline processes.
3. Execute: Fix the fire. Identify what's most broken— the area where fixing it creates the biggest ROI in time, money, or sanity—and create Gameplans and Microplays to solve it.

Once you've built Gameplans, you don't just leave them on a shelf. You assign them. Each Gameplan comes with an owner, and that person is accountable for the outcome it delivers. Not just the task—the outcome. That's execution clarity.

Here's a copy of that visual we started with as a key reminder:

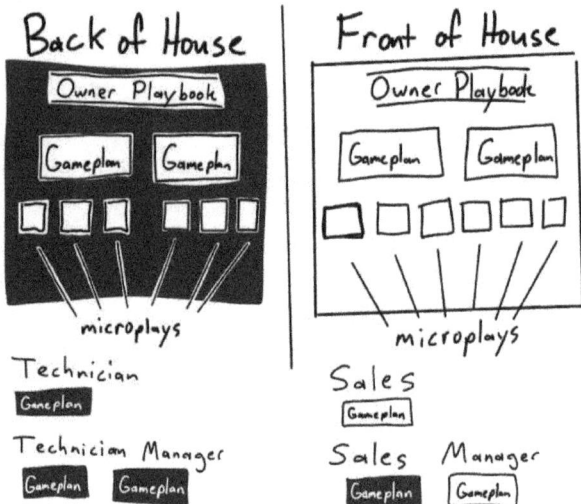

Once you've assigned Gameplans to someone, *they* are in charge of the outcomes for that Gameplan!

Now. . . exactly how are you going to ensure everyone knows all this information? As in, . . . how are you going to get it to them? I got you. Next chapter.

CHAPTER 6

All Things Distribution

"I sold the company?!?" I said. My assistant just laughed. I was astonished. I hadn't sold the company. "The word really was spreading around. The team thought they had seen you for the last time," my assistant said, still laughing (undoubtedly at the look of surprise on my face). Of course I was surprised. I prided myself on the culture and relationship I had built with them, both as a group and on a personal level. I felt like I really knew my people and that they knew me. And now they thought I had up and sold the company. I couldn't understand it. Yes, I'd been working from home, traveling, and taking on other projects, but I'd just been in the office three weeks ago. Something had to change. I couldn't continue to be so disconnected from my company. Every time I worked from home, they worried I was selling.

Around the same time as this was all going down, the usage of the company portal was particularly disappointing. My employees knew about the company portal, but they didn't know all it had to offer. They still assumed it was easier just to ask somebody how to do it or, worse, just wing it. I needed a way to get both my face and my tools in front of my team more regularly.

What followed was a quick-and-dirty system on how to get facetime and distribute our Microplays on a daily, weekly, monthly basis.

In a nutshell:

- Daily: Use daily questions to reply with Microplays. This ensures that people now have the answer to the question they're looking for *and shouldn't need to ask it again.*
- Weekly: Setup a consistent video that gets sent to everyone. This ensures you're making facetime with your employees on a consistent basis.
- Monthly: A once-a-month newsletter is a great way to communicate broader company goals, upcoming milestones, etc.

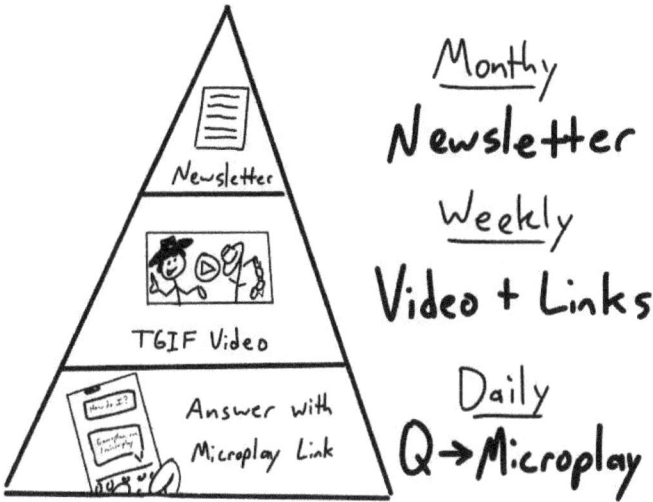

Monthly
Newsletter

Weekly
Video + Links

Daily
Q → Microplay

Distribution

Up to this point, we've discussed how to create Microplays, Gameplans, and Owner's Playbooks. And while those are minimally helpful as documents to whip out in an emergency, they're far more effective when read consistently, communicated widely, and upheld generally.

So, how do we do it? How do we get our well thought-out Microplays and Gameplans into the hands of those who need them most?

Initially, my first thought was to make all the information *attractive*. Before I pushed out my Microplays and Gameplans to my team, I needed them to enjoy, if at all possible, accessing the portal. So, I had a brilliant idea: I moved a compensation calculator to the employee portal so that whenever they wanted to calculate their pay, they had to log in (this is important because we pay piece rate/percentage pay). My thought was that they'd maybe see the Microplays and start using them.

Then, I went further, ensuring that all time-off and inventory requests were processed through the employee portal. Overall, I saw a slight increase in the engagement with the Microplays, but not as much as I wanted. And led me down the path to the following distribution rhythm, which has been a phenomenal tool for many of my coaching clients:

Daily / Ad-Hoc

To distribute Microplays on a daily basis, all I do is answer any questions my staff has with a link to the Microplay that answers it. Not only does this save you time, it also teaches them that the Microplays are a quick way to get access to all the answers they need. When they see how easy and palatable the Microplays and portal are, they'll start to use them to answer their questions instead of interrupting you. Over time, this doesn't just save you from being the bottleneck; it standardizes how we do things company-wide, so everyone is following the same process, the same way, every time.

Weekly

The weekly distribution is where everyone in my company sees my face and hears my voice, which provides security and stability to everyone. This is just a short, three- to five-minute video. Don't overthink it, don't edit it, just make it as easy as possible.

I film what I call a TGIF video, and in it, I discuss a few top questions from the week, which I find by asking each of my managers to send me requests based on current needs. Then, I add in the links to the Microplays to the same message with the TGIF video, so that the answers are only 1 Layer Deep™.

These are a great way to show my personal side to the employees. Once, I filmed the video and sent it out on Friday morning, per usual. A few minutes later, I rewatched the video and, on closer inspection, found that my bra was hanging on the door handle in the background. I wrestled with reshooting the video, but eventually decided to just acknowledge it: "Sorry for the bra in the background." Everyone thought it was hilarious. But more importantly, it showed them that I'm a real person who makes mistakes.

The reason I know the employees are watching and sometimes even looking forward to the videos, though, is because every now and then I forget to post one and get bombarded with messages. "Where is your TGIF dispatch video?" "Hey, Libby, are you OK? I didn't see your video," and even, "Libby! What's going on?" Security. Consistency. Familiarity. Not getting the video on Friday is the same feeling you get when you receive mail every single day, and then one day you don't. Or when your TV show is on at the same time every night and one night it's not. Picture this: You get a new job in a part of town you don't normally travel to. The roads are unfamiliar, and you have some growing pains as you learn the route, but gradually you learn it, nonetheless. Soon enough, you don't even have to think about it; your car might as well be driving itself. But then one day, there is construction. Suddenly, your commute and perhaps your entire day are thrown off. You don't even realize how ingrained and internalized your trip is until you are knocked out of your routine. This is similar to what happens with the dispatch videos. They got so used to the videos and specifically the closing statement that they could recite the core values phrase from memory, and got worried when I didn't post the video.

How big of a difference can it really make if employees hear and repeat these words? Turns out, it makes a huge difference, and there's research to back it up. "The Elderly Study," done in 1996, found that participants who were primed (via scrambled sentence puzzle) with words relating to aging, such as wrinkle, bingo, and Florida, walked more slowly than those who were primed with neutral words. In another study done two years later, researchers found that people of identical intelligence fared better on a test when they were told to think about the word "professor" versus those who were told to think about the phrase "soccer hooligan." Even the US military uses these priming techniques to train soldiers to be more resilient, function better under pressure, and have higher emotional intelligence. Hearing the positive words of our core values every Friday helps my team embody those traits throughout the week. One of the best things you can do for your people is prime them with positive words that will help them be the company you want them to be.

Never bring negative topics to the group. Talking to the group is never the place for pointing fingers. Those are for one-on-ones with your team. If there is a general problem that pertains to everybody, simply talk about the Microplay that is relevant. If you're having a problem with callouts, go over the time off request Microplay.

Monthly

Monthly, I send out a newsletter. I'm not going to explain in any detail how to write a newsletter, but I will explain a few general rules to follow and how to implement the newsletter well. First of all, the newsletter follows some of the same rules as the dispatch video: always positive, never pointing fingers, and links to all the Microplays that are discussed. If something needs to be brought up and can be brought up positively, the newsletter is a good place to do that. I like to choose a "play of the month" to highlight in the newsletter based on what we are struggling with in the company or need to be reminded of.

I have three other sections in addition to this: "What's Happening?," "What's New?," and "What's Next?" The "What's Happening?" section gives a little context to the company about what we are working on at the moment, metrics we've hit recently, etc. The "What's New?" section updates the company on any new Microplays, policies, or any other changes we might make. Finally comes the "What's Next?" section, which keeps the company up to date on our goals and milestones. With this section, the company turns its eyes ahead to the next few months and refocuses on its goals. We make sure to send these out at the beginning of the month so that as we finish up with this section, we leave everyone with a clear idea of the goals for the month. All of this should be about one page of information. Just like the Microplays, we don't want these to drag on. We want them to be engaging and concise. Short, sweet, and to the point.

Pro Tip: Consistency

In all of our distribution and communication of any kind, we need to be consistent. I don't care when you send out your newsletter, or even if it's weekly or bi-monthly, be consistent. If you're going to send your newsletter out on the thirty-first, send it out on the thirty-first. There must be a rhythm; without rhythm, an orchestra only produces cacophony. (If you've ever been to an elementary school band concert, you know what I mean!) If an orchestra has rhythm, though, all of the instruments work together smoothly and create a *symphony*. In the same way, our commandeered businesses must have rhythm and consistency to work together smoothly and produce fruitful results. The distribution rhythm is like the percussion; it's the heartbeat of the company.

On to Part II: LESS LAYERS, MORE RESULTS

So, we've made (or swipe!) Microplays for your business. We've fought the fires, mapped your roles, and even dealt, a bit, with yourself.

Now, it's time to start cutting through the other layers of B.S. that often attach themselves to our ego, our processes, and our business just when we're trying to make momentum. In the next chapters, we're going to take a battle ax to any and every area that is causing unnecessary friction in your business (and personal life). Let's get to it!

PART II

LESS LAYERS.
MORE RESULTS.

1 Layer Deep™

CHAPTER 7

The Five Ego Buckets

In 2021, my husband, Chris, was working as COO of my recruiting software, WootRecruit. One day, we were sitting down to eat breakfast at our kitchen table when I noticed he seemed... off. He said it was nothing, so I left it alone. As we ate, I noticed he kept checking his phone and typing out messages on it. I had a feeling whatever was bothering him was work-related, so I checked my company's main Slack channel for any updates. Nothing. On a hunch, I did a quick search of *all* the channels. Bingo. In every channel, people had been tagging my husband with their questions.

"Chris, why are they asking you all these questions?" I asked.

"Well ... I'm the only one who knows how to do what they're asking."

"Don't you have any of this stuff documented?"

"I haven't gotten around to it yet. . ."

After I'd taught so many people to document their answers and given dozens of talks on not answering the same questions, here was Chris doing that very thing. We had made hundreds of Microplays for our companies; we even had Microplays for chores around the house. Before I guilt-tripped him, I looked into his face. He looked miserable.

"You understand you're setting yourself up for this, right?" I asked as gently as I could. "You're going to turn this job into one that you hate."

He nodded glumly.

I asked him one last question: "Are you answering questions to feel important?"

He shook his head. "Of course not! I feel miserable! Why would I do this to myself *intentionally*?"

I caught a final glance of him before he headed to start work, and honestly, he looked like a man who already hated his job.

Later, Chris came back to me. "You were right. I've been thinking about what you said all day. I didn't even realize it, but I enjoy being the answer guy. It feels good to be the only person who knows how to get the job done. I *was* setting myself up for this."

I smiled. I had been there, so many times myself, wanting to be the hero.

Imagine you are sitting on the bank of a river and you see someone drowning. You dive into the water and haul the drowning person to shore. You would be considered a hero. But now, imagine you felt so good about saving the person that you sit on the riverbank every day, waiting for someone to start drowning so you can save them. That's not a healthy way to find significance, but it's exactly what many of us business owners do. And it makes sense: Neuroscience shows that when people feel needed, their brains light up in ways that increase motivation, happiness, and even physical health. For instance, in the 1970s, researchers conducted a study on nursing home patients. Each patient received a plant. Half were given the responsibility of keeping the plant alive. The other half were told the staff would look after their plants. By the end of the study, the researchers noted how many patients were living. Soberingly, twice as many people from the group given charge over their plants were alive. While this study is a bit morbid, it shows just how important it is to feel needed.[14]

The trick is to feel needed without having to be the person standing on the riverbank waiting for someone to drown. A better place to find significance than being the "answer guy" or "answer girl," is from your personal relationships, with

---

[14] https://www.modernpeople.com.au/articles/the-science-of-mattering-why-feeling-significant-is-so-significant

family or friends, or even colleagues from work. Or, if you really feel significance from solving dire problems, why not, again, *focus on solutions,* instead of waiting for (or subconsciously recreating!) the scenarios that first caused the emergency in the first place?

The Five Ego Buckets

Chris had fallen into one of the five ego buckets, each starting with a need:

1) Need for significance
2) Need for chaos
3) Need for perfection
4) Need for acceptance
5) Need for familiarity

It's important to know which bucket, because knowing which bucket we're in helps us get out. So, in this chapter, we'll unpack each one. In case you're wondering, *What does this have to do with* 1 Layer Deep™*?* Well, I'll tell you:

Remember that the basic 1 Layer Deep™ method is Align, Delete, Execute. And Delete means simply to cut out the B.S. that's keeping you or someone else from the final step to the solution they're looking for. And oftentimes, the B.S. that needs to get cut is our emotional or psychological noise.

1: Need for Significance

This is the one Chris was struggling with—the need to be the answer guy, or the answer girl. Chris's problem wasn't so much that he didn't *trust* his team to get the work done right. His problem was that it felt good to be the person they came to when they needed help.

People who struggle with this need have a desire to feel smart, important, or needed.

Again, take it back to parenting: Moms often feel a loss of identity as their child starts getting older and becoming more independent. Even though they know that growth is a natural part of human progression, it hurts to feel less needed. So, many moms fight against this by doing everything for their growing child, and, intentionally or inadvertently, they often stunt their child's own personal development.

Business owners and even management often wrestle with a similar (although slightly less intimate) version of the same: Simply put, they don't want to feel unneeded. So, they (often subconsciously) make themselves critical for everyday operations. What they don't realize (or often ignore) is that employee autonomy is essential for company growth. In any healthy organization—in a family, a nonprofit, or a business—growing individuals should constantly become more and more self-reliant. Does this mean that the owner won't have a part in their lives anymore? No! It just means the owner will have more free time and energy to interact with employees directly, and on a more personal level. Michael Scott, the fictional character from *The Office* who's the regional manager of Dunder-Mifflin Paper Company, is hilariously a great example of a manager working effectively: Throughout the entire show, Michael does little to no work in regard to the organization, and yet, their branch is recognized as one of the most successful in the company. His team is almost completely autonomous. Scott has a lot of free time because of this and uses it to engage with his people and develop a strong culture and relationships with them. In my own business, I've learned to be like Michael Scott. I can now proactively develop the culture of my business. I'm now able to have more meaningful interaction with my team members, and I even hold monthly one-on-ones with each person.

Just like a parent's goal is to develop their child into an independent, successful adult, your goal is to grow your business and organize it so that it thrives *without* you. This doesn't mean you have to lose your connection with your team. What it means is you can now have an even stronger connection with them that isn't centered around the little day-to-day things.

Note: This Need doesn't only apply to owners: Chris wasn't even the owner of the company, and he still fell into this bucket. Maybe you're not the answer guy or answer girl, but you might have somebody in your company who is. Case in point: stop being the hero. Be like Michael.

2: Need for Chaos

"You're setting up your whole team to fail," I said, slightly exasperated. I was coaching a client (we'll call her Jane) who was self-sabotaging. Jane seemed intent on not changing her ways. "There's no way they are going to succeed in this environment," I concluded.

"But... I like it."

"You like it because you're an entrepreneur. We *thrive* on chaos. We are addicted to the adrenaline: It makes us feel alive. Our employees, on the other hand, hate it. They need stability in the workplace."

Jane's story highlights an uncomfortable truth: Statistically, most entrepreneurs grow up in chaotic lifestyles. As a result, most of us are good—too good—at working, and even *thriving*, in chaos. Instead of enjoying the stability, many owners unconsciously inject chaos back into the business—changing directions mid-project, chasing a shiny new idea, redoing work that was already done. It creates drama where none existed, just to feel that familiar rush again.

The problem is, what feels energizing for the owner is exhausting for the team. Employees see it as sabotage—because, in practice, that's what it is.

Entrepreneurs in this category suffer the same fate as what most of us would call "adrenaline junkies." Jane had created a volatile workspace so that she would have problems to solve.

How to Stop Self-Sabotaging

The Need for Chaos is so prevalent among entrepreneurs, I wanted to highlight a specific tool I have for tackling this one. You'll need to regularly audit yourself for self-destructive habits. Ideally, you do this with a spouse or partner (or a trusted entrepreneur), and hold each other accountable by asking each other these questions:

- Did you self-sabotage since we last met?
- What was the context before you did?
- What were you thinking the *moment* you self-sabotaged?

- What are the things you could have told yourself in that moment before you acted?
- Is there a daily practice you can put in place to overcome this tendency?

Simple questions, but these will drive *huge* results, trust me!

Personal Note

Chris and I actually do this together. On our couples quarterly, we sat down and wrote out the ways we self-sabotage. For me, it came down to two habits: overcommitting and procrastination. My favorite line used to be, "I'm not ready yet." It made me feel better in the moment—like I had a good reason to delay. But really, it was just me avoiding the work.

I asked Chris to call me out anytime he heard me say it. And let me tell you—it's uncomfortable having your partner catch you in the act. But it worked. Suddenly, I couldn't hide behind the excuse. I had to move. And when I started moving, I realized how much faster and lighter things felt.

That's why I push so hard on this point: self-sabotage is sneaky. Most of the time, you don't even see it in yourself until someone holds up a mirror. That's the real value of doing this audit with a spouse, partner, or trusted peer—they'll spot your blind spots and won't let you off the hook.

3: Need for Perfection

Many entrepreneurs, especially female owners, struggle with perfectionism. For us, if it's getting done, it's getting done the right way. The negative flip side of this is if it's not going to be perfect, then we won't do it. We are afraid that we'll mess it up. I call this Perfectionism Paralysis. If we can't do it the right way now, then we'll wait until we can do it the right way. The problem is, this freezes up the entire business. We can no longer grow if we don't continue to innovate, create, and improve the way we do things to be more productive.

Helicopter owners fit into many buckets simultaneously, but the Need for Perfection is *huge* with helicopter owners: They do their teams' jobs for them, whether that be answering questions or physically completing tasks.

Owners who suffer from this Need micromanage everyone because they don't trust them to do as good of a job as the owner, which of course, is probably true: No one will ever care about getting the job done right as much as you do— because you're the owner. But that's the problem: you can't possibly have the time and energy to do *everything* for your company. You must delegate or you won't be able to grow. As Theodore Roosevelt said, "The best executive is the one who has sense enough to pick good men to do what he wants done, and self-restraint enough to keep from meddling with them while they do it."[15]

---

[15] https://www.forbes.com/quotes/8958/

> "The best executive is the one who has sense enough to pick good men to do what he wants done, and self-restraint enough to keep from meddling with them while they do it."

Understanding my own mistrust was one of my biggest unlocks. Starting out, I thought I was the only one that could do the job right. I was a total control freak. When I learned to let go, the feeling after the weight lifted from my shoulders was incredible. And you're not just checking out like a Carrie Underwood song and praying for Jesus to take the wheel; there's a proper way to retain control and ensure standard quality is met without having to be involved in every single decision and task. That's what the rest of the book is about, but if you want the quick and dirty answer, it's this:

Documentation.

You need to document every task you want done and ensure the people responsible for that task know they're responsible for it.

4: Need for Acceptance

One of the main drivers behind the Need for Perfection is the fear of being judged by others, so these two are entirely related. Many of us, (again, I'm looking at my female founders) are scared of looking like we don't know what we're doing. We're scared we won't look like "the boss." We're terrified of failing. We're constantly comparing ourselves to our counterparts, male or female. The reality is that we judge ourselves more than anyone else judges us. The truth is, asking for help isn't a sign of weakness—it's the sign of a strong leader.

We must get over the fear of failing. Failing is a natural part of growth. Albert Einstein hit it on the nose (as he often does) when he said, "Failure is success in progress." When learning to ride your bike, you shouldn't expect to never fall off. On the contrary, you should expect to fall off pretty frequently, for a while. But as you fail over and over, you're on a journey that ends with you being able to ride your bike with little to no thought or effort. "Every 'no' brings you closer to a 'yes,'" is a common phrase in the sales industry, penned by Mark Cuban. What it means is that if you keep trying and failing again and again, eventually, you will succeed.

I say all this to change the way we think about failing. Even with the oversaturation of "fail-then-succeed" content currently out there, we're still scared of failing, and are embarrassed by it. I emphasize that failure is natural because learning to get over that fear is essential. Failure is an opportunity to learn much faster than if you hadn't.

A running joke in my company is my spelling. I can't spell to save my life. Whenever I'm on a live call with my teams, and I'm sharing my screen, more than a few jokes get cracked.

When I was first starting out as a business leader, this may have been detrimental to my self-confidence. However, as I've grown as a person and a leader, I've learned not to be embarrassed by my shortcomings (we now call them "Libby-isms").

Borrowed Confidence

If you're wrestling with yourself about whether or not you can do this, you can. You may have heard of the term "borrowed confidence," a tool to use when you don't have the confidence to do something by using someone else's confidence in your ability. So, borrow my belief in you. I know that if a random half-Native-American, half-Mexican girl from Oklahoma with no formal education can do it, you can too.

5: Need for Familiarity

This bucket disguises itself as humility. The owners who fall into it usually have some kind of idea that they don't deserve success. While this philosophy may appear as humility, it's really a lack of self-confidence and clear goals, and you'll need both to resolve this Need:

- **Self-confidence:** Owners must believe they can achieve what they want to achieve. As cheesy as it sounds, if you can't believe in yourself, how can anyone else?

As Eleanor Roosevelt (and yes, I realize I've quoted two Roosevelts in the same chapter) said: "No man is defeated without until he has first been defeated within." It's like learning to ride a bike: We start out with a high degree of self-doubt, but we give it a go anyway. Initially, we're still very wobbly, but we're moving forward. From there, two outcomes are possible: you doubt yourself and succumb to the wobble and gravity, or you defy gravity and friction, pedaling harder despite your doubt, gaining fluidity as you gain momentum.

If we defy our doubts and push through to the other side, we will find that working towards and achieving our goals is as easy as riding a bike.

- **Clarify goals:** The other thing we must have are clear goals. If we can't envision where we're trying to ride our bike, and all the steps required to get there, it's going to be much harder to arrive. The principle is the same in our businesses. We must have clearly defined, specific goals, ones that stretch our current capabilities (entrepreneurs *need* challenges!). We'll talk more about goals, how to build them, and why they are essential in later chapters.

People who struggle with these two elements are worried because they don't know how to be the successful person who has achieved all of their goals. But the truth is, by the time you get there, being that person will come naturally to you. You won't have to worry about knowing what a successful person would do because you are the successful person. The goals we set are crucial here because they decide what limits us. If we set low goals because of our fears or doubts, then we will reach them comfortably but never grow. We grow when we set goals that are *barely* attainable and go all-in on achieving them. That's where self-confidence is built.

Personal Note: Walking Without Anchors

There's another layer to this idea of self-confidence that I call fearlessness. Fearlessness isn't about believing everything will work out—that's faith, and faith still leans on something outside of you, some anchor you're holding onto. Fearlessness is different. It's what happens when you strip away all those anchors and step forward anyway.

For me, fearlessness has looked like walking straight through fires I wasn't sure I'd survive—not because I knew the outcome, but because standing still wasn't an option. Every time, I had to release the beacons that would have pulled me back: titles, certainty, reputation. And I had to trust myself to keep moving.

It's not easy. But when you stop leaning on external anchors and walk through anyway, you come out sharper, stronger, and more capable of standing on your own when things get rough. That's fearlessness—and it's one of the most important muscles you can build as a business owner.

Learning to Be Self-Aware

Most entrepreneurs fall into one of the ego buckets, especially if they're not consciously working not to. You may fall into any of the Five, and you'll probably connect with one of them more than the others. Don't disregard the rest of this section because you only relate to one; chances are, you just haven't fallen into the others *yet*. And yes, I get it, dealing with egos is difficult, as everything today is catered to our ego. We use social media to collect likes and followers. Salesmen know to say our names because each of us enjoys the sound of them. But the stakes are high: At the end of the day, every one of these ego buckets can and will affect the organization of your business, how you run your business, and how productive your daily operations are. If you keep handling the day-to-day functions because of your ego:

a) It's all you'll ever be good at

b) You will never dig out of your hole of day-to-day monotony

c) You and your business will never reach its full potential

The good news? Awareness is half the battle. Just acknowledging that your ego is interfering with your life and business is a huge step. You now have the capability to be on guard against it as you are considering where to go from here. The next steps depend on your ego bucket. Whether you need to borrow confidence, create stronger goals and get pedaling, start a new venture, or create the culture and relationship with your team that you've always wanted, is up to you. The one thing that you must keep in mind with every ego bucket is the objective: for your business to run smoothly, efficiently, successfully, and autonomously. If we lose sight of that principle, then we're halfway to hating our job. If we can keep it in mind then we can achieve whatever goals we set for ourselves and our team.

Self-Check: Ask "Why?"

The first step is to understand what bucket you're in; the next, is to deal with it. And that path starts with asking "why?" multiple times.

With Chris, I first asked him why he was getting asked so many questions. When he told me he wasn't documenting answers, I again asked why. Eventually, he came back with an honest answer: he liked being the answer guy. This told us that he fell into the bucket of Need for Significance.

From there, it's up to you to decide how far to go with the why game. If you think there is a deeper problem, you can take the why game all the way back to your childhood. Not all cases of ego need to go back there, but it can be extremely beneficial and sometimes crucial.

Self-Check: Ask "Why?"

- **Step 1: Write down your first answer.**

- **Step 2: Ask "Why?" again.**

- **Step 3: Keep climbing until you hit the root cause.**

  (Most answers take at least 3–5 Whys.)

1 Layer Deep™ Personal Application

Protecting Your Kingdom

If you've ever tried to run a business while your personal life was chaotic, you know the two are inseparable. The health of your home and your inner world directly mirror the health of your business. You can't have one organized and the other in shambles—it always leaks through.

When I think about ego and personal life, I think of a kingdom. You are that kingdom. And like any kingdom, you have walls and rings that protect what's inside. From the outer walls where outsiders come in, to the inner courtyards where family and close relationships live, all the way to the throne at the very center—where you sit as royalty. That's where the hardest work happens, because that's where you face yourself.

Let's walk through the kingdom, ring by ring.

The Outer Wall

The outer walls are where outsiders interact with your home life. This could be the lawn crew, pool cleaner, nanny, housekeeper, or contractor. Delegation is good: It frees you to focus on what matters. But many of us bring people into our kingdom and then micromanage them to death. Instead of creating peace, we create a middleman between us and the task.

When this happens, it's rarely about the task itself. It's usually one of the ego buckets showing up—often the Need for Perfection or Need for Significance. If you truly want your kingdom secure, you've got to trust the people you've brought inside the walls. Otherwise, you're just standing guard all day instead of ruling.

The Courtyard

Inside the walls are your family and your closest friends. This is the heart of the kingdom. But here's the hard reality: many people share a roof but aren't truly doing life together. Living together and building a life together are two different things.

You can't run a healthy business and have an unhealthy home. That doesn't always mean marriage—it means stability. If you go from a stressful business straight into a chaotic household, you won't last long. Your kingdom will eventually crumble.

This is also where friends matter. Who you allow into the courtyard influences the culture of your kingdom. If they bring drama, you'll live with drama. If they bring encouragement, you'll live with encouragement. Studies prove this—your habits, happiness, even your health are shaped by the people closest to you. Audit who gets access to your courtyard, because your kingdom will reflect their influence.

The Throne Room

And then there's the throne—the center of the kingdom. That's you. This is where the work stings the most, because this is where you confront the truth: if you don't grow personally, your business and your family will eventually outgrow you.

This isn't just about hobbies or self-care (though those matter). It's about asking deeper questions:

- What am I really trying to achieve?
- What's my purpose?
- Why do I do all of this?

This is what I call your "third mountain." The first two are building your business and developing yourself. The third is figuring out who you are without the business. If your identity is only tied to your company, it's fragile. Because what happens when the business fails? Or worse, what happens when it no longer needs you?

A true king or queen doesn't find their identity in the walls or the courtyards. They find it in the ability to sit alone on the throne and know they belong there. That's what ego work looks like when you apply it 1 Layer Deep™.

Pro Tip: Business is the Vehicle, Not the Vessel

Our business is not supposed to be the vessel that defines who we are. It's the vehicle that helps us get where we're going. There's a big difference.

When we treat the business like the vessel, we put all of our identity and purpose inside of it. That feels good in the moment, but it doesn't last. At some point, the business won't need us in the same way, or the business may even fail. If it's been our vessel, then when it moves on without us, we're left with nothing.

I've been there. I hit the million-dollar mark in my cleaning company, then doubled it, expecting that the success would finally feel different. It didn't. I had been expecting the business to carry me when in reality, it was only meant to move me forward. A business can give you money, time, and freedom, but it can't tell you why those things matter. That has to come from you.

This is where the third mountain comes in. The first mountain is building the business. The second is building yourself—your skills, your leadership, your ability to grow. The third mountain is your purpose. That's where you stop asking, "What number am I trying to hit?" and start asking, "Why am I climbing at all?"

As your business becomes more autonomous and you get time and energy back, that space has to go somewhere. Some of it will go back into the business, but it can't all stay there. Some of it has to go into you—into clarifying your goals, into finding your identity, into deciding what matters most. That's how you keep the business as the vehicle instead of the vessel.

The same thing applies at home. It's easy to say you want to be free and spontaneous there, but structure doesn't box you in. It frees you. The responsibilities and tasks are going to exist no matter what. You can either set them up so they're handled without constant involvement, or you can spend your life putting out fires.

When you're aligned with your family and friends, and your goals are clear, you're not weighed down. You're supported. And when your sense of purpose and identity are anchored outside of the business, you're on solid ground. Your happiness and fulfillment don't rise and fall with the company. They come from you.

∧∧∧

CHAPTER 8

The 3 Cs to Eliminating Inefficiencies

Forty-one minutes per week. That's how much time my head of marketing (whom we'll call Lucinda) was spending managing the team. Forty-one minutes. I tried to find an activity that people spend such a small amount of time doing, but I couldn't. We spend more time reading, playing video games, even going to the bathroom. Forty-one minutes a week is about eight minutes a day. Not only was she wasting tons of time, (the other 2,359 minutes per week, to be exact) but I was paying her top dollar, too. She was the highest-paid person in the company, aside from me. I hired her because of her qualifications. Lucinda came from a big company, and she checked all the boxes (on paper). We soon found out that, while she may have looked good on paper, her work ethic was subpar. She worked with us for eight months, and towards the end, my husband and I were hardly getting to see our kids because we were so busy doing her job for her.

The worst part is that's not the only time this has happened. I had another head of marketing in another of my companies named Alvin, who did the same thing a few years back. In fact, this has happened numerous times. I've spent somewhere between $800,000 and $900,000 on these 'expensive learning experiences'. I blame myself for these mistakes; it was my oversight that let the problem persist for so long, and my vetting at the interview that let them happen in the first place. The thing is, these mistakes are bound to happen. The first interview is like going on a first date. You can tell a lot about the person, but there's also a lot you won't see. Chris (my husband) has a theory that applicants oversell themselves by 150 to 200 percent in the interview. While this is based on our personal experience, a survey in 2023 showed that 70 percent of applicants reported lying on their resume, with 37 percent saying they did it frequently[16]. This is important because it shows that there are going to be mistakes and we are going to miss things in the interview that we'll wish we had seen. When we inevitably hire a suboptimal employee, we end up paying them more money for the same amount of work. We hire them to do a job that's

---

[16] Paola Peralta, "Recruiters Beware: 70% of Employees Say They've Lied on Their Resumes," Employee Benefit News, October 5, 2023, https://www.benefitnews.com/news/resumelab-found-that-70-of-workers-admit-to-lying-on-their-resume-heres-why.

worth $20 per hour, but then they end up taking twice as long as needed to do that job. Now we're really paying them $40 per hour for work that a better hire could have done in half as much time. This adds up over the course of our career (see the part where I lost almost a million dollars because of this, albeit on a larger scale). Before you buy back your time, you need to make sure you're not buying back inefficiencies.

A similar situation: the fall in productivity among our current employees. In the natural progression of a company, employee efficiency and productivity declines over time. Maybe your team gets comfortable and starts slacking off a little bit. Maybe they gradually drift away from the procedures you started them out with. Whatever the reason, they're not as time-effective as they once were. Or maybe they were never efficient in the first place. You might be thinking that the difference is probably negligible, right? Wrong. Research shows people spend ninety minutes a day *just task-switching.* To put this into perspective 90 minutes per day, 5 days per week, 52 weeks per year is 23,400 minutes. That's 390 hours per year. At an assumed hourly rate of $20 for mid-level office staff, your 390 hours of wasted time is costing you $7,800 a year alone in task-switching. Per person. Multiply that by the number of employees you have, and you'll understand why I say this is a big deal (to go even further, you can multiply that by the average hourly rate of your employees and see the dollar amount that it is costing you).

$$\frac{\text{Context Switching Cost}}{\begin{array}{l} 90 \text{ min}/\text{day} \\ \times \ 5 \text{ days}/\text{wk.} \\ \times \ 52 \text{ wks}/\text{yr} \end{array}}$$

$$= 23,400 \text{ min}$$

aka: 390 HOURS/yr

aka: $\$7,800$ per yr/employee
(at an assumed $\$20$/hr)

As you can see, we are losing thousands of hours and hundreds of thousands of dollars, both because of entropy within our businesses and because of mistakes in the hiring process. If these things are having such a negative impact on our business, how can we eliminate these losses? To get rid of problems like this with our interviews and onboarding, we can try to nail down our hiring processes (something I've spent years doing). To get rid of the inefficiencies, we can have mandatory refresher courses on protocol to try and keep our people on the straight and narrow. Both of these are important and can help, but to be completely frank, there is no way to eliminate these problems. We're not going to be able to completely rid our company of wastes of time and resources. This can be a daunting thing to face, especially for those of us who are perfectionists. What keeps me sane is the fact that over the many years spent and employees hired, I've *only* lost $800,000 to $900,000. I've known many who have spent much more than that. They hire an expensive manager and find out a couple hundred thousand dollars and months later that they weren't qualified for the job (and that the department they were managing is on fire). The key is to minimize the losses you take. After years of taking these massive hits to my budget, I've developed a streamlined, simple process for ruthlessly fighting inefficiencies and squandered profits. I call it the 3 Cs to Finding Inefficiencies: Capture, Cultivate, and Crystallize. By following this method, I not only find the places where my team has strayed from the beaten path to a less effective route (Capture), but I also consistently improve on the established processes and procedures (Cultivate). Not only this, when push comes to shove, I've been able to make the tough calls on whether or not someone is adding to the business or holding it back (Crystallize). By doing this, I've saved $100,000+ ... in two weeks. The 3 Cs to Inefficiencies will change the standard for efficiency in your business. [17]

Capturing Inefficiencies

Time that we spend idly tends to be stealthy. It slinks around the edges of our thoughts; we don't feel guilty about a specific thing, instead, we feel undirected shame. At the end of the day, we look back and wonder where we spent all twenty-four hours. We spend a little bit of time doing the most important things and spend the rest either transitioning

---

[17] We started an entire company, WootRecruit, just to handle process problems like this!

between things (driving, walking, preparing to do something) or avoiding doing the important things (scrolling on our phones, playing games, skirting the issues). To be productive, we have to stay alert to the little ways time slips through the cracks. It doesn't usually disappear in big chunks; it leaks out in minutes here and there until the day is gone. That's why the first C of the 3Cs, Capture, is all about noticing where those leaks happen. Once we see them clearly, we can plug the holes.

The tool I use for this is the time audit sheet. It's simple, but it works. Every year in every one of my companies, we run time audits to see where effort is being wasted, where transitions are dragging too long, or where distractions are creeping in. Once those patterns are on paper, we can "capture" the inefficiencies before they quietly drain our profits dry.

The way it works: each employee makes a copy of the spreadsheet. It looks something like this.

Date	Activity	Start:	Finish:	Total Time	Anyone / Multiple / Only me	
					1 / 2 / 3	☐
					1 / 2 / 3	☐
					1 / 2 / 3	☐
					1 / 2 / 3	☐
					1 / 2 / 3	☐
					1 / 2 / 3	☐
					1 / 2 / 3	☐
					1 / 2 / 3	☐
					1 / 2 / 3	☐
					1 / 2 / 3	☐
					1 / 2 / 3	☐
					1 / 2 / 3	☐
					1 / 2 / 3	☐
					1 / 2 / 3	☐
					1 / 2 / 3	☐
					1 / 2 / 3	☐
					1 / 2 / 3	☐
					1 / 2 / 3	☐
					1 / 2 / 3	☐
					1 / 2 / 3	☐
					1 / 2 / 3	☐
					1 / 2 / 3	☐

+ ≡ | Day 1 | Day 2 | Day 3 | Day 4 | Day 5 |

For each activity they do or task they complete, they should put the date, a detailed description of the activity or task, the time they started and finished the activity or task, and the time they spent on it. Then they should select whether the activity or task was something anyone could do, something a handful of people could do, or something only they could do. They will do this for every task that they do during a full work week. Once it's completed, it should look like this.

Date	Activity	Start:	Finish:	Total Time	Anyone/Multiple/Only me	
06/25	~~~~~~	8:04 am	8:10 am	6:00	1	□
06/25	~~~~~~	8:11 am	8:12 am	1:00	1	☑
06/25	~~~~~~	8:12 am	8:27 am	15:00	1	□
06/25	~~~~~~	8:28 am	8:31 am	3:00	1	□
06/25	~~~~~~	8:32 am	8:34 am	2:00	1	□
06/25	~~~~~~	8:34 am	9:00 am	26:00	1	☑
06/25	~~~~~~	9:00 am	9:14 am	14:00	1	□
06/25	~~~~~~	9:14 am	9:24 am	10:00	1	□
06/25	~~~~~~	9:27 am	9:30 am	3:00	1	□
06/25	~~~~~~	9:30 am	9:32 am	2:00	1	□
06/25	~~~~~~	9:33 am	9:34 am	1:00	1	□
						□
						□
						□
						□
						□
						□
						□
						□
						□
						□
						□

+ ≡ | Day 1 | Day 2 | Day 3 | Day 4 | Day 5 |

By the time your employees have filled this out, both of you should understand where they're being productive... and where they're not.

Pro Tip: Visualizing the TVA

To get an even better visual of the time they are spending, you can use AI to do a Time Value Assessment. This will give you a graph showing what percentage of their time they are spending on general categories. To see an example prompt, go to https://1layerdeep.com/resources

Not only will this motivate you, but they will probably feel the pressure to change as well. That's one of the benefits of the time audit sheet: everyone is perfectly clear on what areas need improvement. In my companies, I take this to the next level. I make all of the time audit sheets public and visible to the team. While this isn't a requirement for everyone reading this book, I've found that it adds an extra layer of accountability that is very helpful. I even put my time audit sheet on display to give myself that accountability. You heard it right: I do a time audit for myself as well. It's not just an effective tool for my team; I've captured hours and hours of wasted time in my own schedule. Sometimes I'll look back at it and find that I spent an hour and a half looking for a file. As degrading and painful as it is, I would rather see how much time I'm throwing away and fix it than ignore it.

Not a Performance Review

This can be a depressing thing to look at, for you, but also for your team. We must make sure that they understand that *this is not a performance review*. This is not to judge their ability to do the job. This is simply a tool to find inefficiencies. That's it. We are not even making a better schedule yet (that will be in the next step). The only two things the time audit is used for are 1) shining a light on our daily schedules and finding the places that can be refined, and 2) developing KPIs and job expectations. You can use those KPIs and job expectations to conduct performance reviews later; the time audit is not the time or the place. It is simply a way to get an unbiased view of what's going on in the day-to-day. It may make you feel uncomfortable, like you're invading their privacy or micromanaging. Haven't we been talking about how unsustainable being a helicopter owner is this whole time? The difference is, you're not doing their job for them, you're giving them the tools they need to do their job better, alleviate stress from their daily lives, and be more productive and fulfilled. It's a common practice to record your employees' computer screens to make sure they are staying on task. The time audit accomplishes a similar goal, without the negative messages. When you record their screens, it says you don't trust them, not only to do their work, but also to be honest in reporting how much work they are doing. I don't want to hire people I mistrust like that. I would much rather hire people who I think will be honest about what they are doing and earnestly try to do their job to the best of their ability, even trying to improve. One way I show this is by using the time audit sheets. This gives my employees the opportunity to be honest with me and with themselves about what they're really spending their time on. Now we're working cooperatively; instead of employer against employees, it's employer and employee fighting the inefficiencies together. From there, it's our joint mission to rid their schedule of the fat and streamline their day. The time audit rallies the owner and team member against the common enemy: inefficiencies.

Cultivate: The DITLO (*Day in the Life Of...*) Interview

Now that we have captured a picture of where time is being spent, there are two broad questions we need answered:

1) Why is the employee spending their time this way? When searching for the answer to this question, we often uncover a lack of clarity in procedures, too many distractions, or hidden bottlenecks that are slowing them down.

2) How can we help you do better? By asking this question, we not only show we care about our team, but we also find the hidden superpowers that they have. We all work better in some environments better than others, at some times better than others, and with some people better than with others. These are the kinds of things we look for when answering this question.

The best way to answer these questions is the Day in the Life Of interview—what we call the DITLO: a one-on-one dialogue between a neutral party (often yourself, a manager you've trained, or another leader who can approach the conversation without bias) and an employee.

The message that it sends, the culture that it builds, the practical problems it solves, the hidden surprises it reveals; these things are unmatched by other tools. The first step of the 3Cs, capturing inefficiencies, exposes all of the imperfections in a schedule or routine. This step, cultivating, perfects those imperfections. It takes the information you've found and uses it along with input from the employee to create a much more streamlined process. Where the time audit tore down, the DITLO builds up. It shows your employee that you care about them and want to set them up to do their best work.

A 2024 study found that "Only 30 percent of employees strongly agree that someone at work encourages their development—down from 36 percent in early 2020."

Furthermore, in a recent survey,[18] 71 percent of employees said they would be less likely to leave their current organization if they were recognized more. It's also been found that, "Employees who don't feel recognized are twice as likely to consider leaving within a year..." The numbers speak for themselves: connecting personally with and cultivating your team has a huge impact and can affect your turnover rate in a big way.

Along the same lines: through the DITLO, you can figure out what's keeping them from being their best selves. You're not only clarifying what they did wrong and recognizing what they did right, but you're also receiving feedback from them on what's going on. This isn't just to make them feel heard; it's a practical way of finding and removing obstacles that are holding them back.

For example: Nicki was an employee who wore a lot of hats. You might have called her a tech assistant, but her actual day-to-day was all over the map. She was bouncing between software, downloading and uploading files, creating marketing copy for reels and podcasts (which wasn't her

[18] Jim Harter, "U.S. Employee Engagement Sinks to 10-Year Low," Gallup.com, March 25, 2025, https://www.gallup.com/workplace/654911/employee-engagement-sinks-year-low.aspx.; Christopher Pappas, "Job Satisfaction Statistics: Key Data and Insights in 2025," eLearning Industry, March 26, 2025, https://elearningindustry.com/job-satisfaction-statistics-key-data-and-insights?.; Rebecca Mattina, "20 Employee Recognition Statistics for HR," Achievers, August 14, 2025, https://www.achievers.com/blog/employee-recognition-statistics/.

strength), and handling these tasks one by one as they came up. She was good at organization and time management, so she managed to keep things moving, but the foundation wasn't solid. She wasn't working in a way that maximized her capabilities or her potential to deliver at a higher level.

Her video content, on the other hand, was fantastic. She had a natural eye and talent for it. But because she was bogged down with copywriting and constant adjustments, that strength was getting diluted.

In her DITLO, this became clear. Nicki wasn't failing—she was simply spread too thin across areas that didn't align with her fire. Once we saw it, the solution wasn't to pile on more structure or keep patching over inefficiencies. It was to let her focus on what she did best: producing great video content. We realigned her role to match that fire and she not only became more productive, but far more fulfilled. Her output increased tenfold along with the value she brought to the company (and her self-confidence).

The same way that we have specific things that we, as owners, specialize in, our employees have areas of expertise that we might be overlooking. When I was reviewing time audits, I noticed an interesting trend: some of my guys were very efficient when the task was technical; but when the task wasn't on a computer, they were as slow as molasses. When I brought this up in the DITLO, they all said they were ex-gamers. That explained their prowess in the digital realm. Now, instead of avoiding hiring gamers and buying into the stereotype that gamers are lazy and immature, I seek out gamers for technical positions. We can take our businesses to the next level when we uncover and strategically place people in their flame.

Without the clarity from the DITLO, both Nicki and my gamers could have been written off as "inefficient" or "not good enough," and the default assumption would have been that they were the problem. But they weren't. The issue was not seeing how their roles were misaligned. We can't even begin to imagine the amount of lost opportunity businesses suffer because employees are placed in the wrong roles, their true potential overlooked, and never having the opportunity to prove themselves when they're in their fire.

Cultivation is an essential step in the 3 Cs. This is where change really comes from. By showing our employees that we care and that we're here to help them along the way, we motivate them to be the best they can be and do the best they can do for the company. This step can take a group of individuals who just work together and transform them into one body, all working towards a common goal. We'll talk more about how to rally everyone behind the process and vision in Chapter 9 when we discuss Process Maps.

Pro Tip: Don't Judge

The key to doing the day-in-the-life interview with a family member is being unbiased and non-judgmental. If you come across as judgmental, a) you're not helping anybody get better, and b) you're probably not going to get straight, honest answers. If you're too close to the issue or are more passionate about these things, it will definitely be better to have someone else be the interviewer.

The only thing different from doing a Day in the Life in the business versus doing it with your family is that with your loved ones, a Day in the Life *should always be voluntary*. When we did this for my son, he had specifically requested for us to do one with him. Because this is an established tool in our family, and we'd created a safe environment that encourages vulnerability, my son wasn't embarrassed to ask for help.

Crystallize: Apply Pressure, Make Diamonds

All diamonds... are built under pressure

At this point in the process of the 3 Cs, we've given our employee everything they need to succeed. We've revealed where the inefficiencies are using the time audit. Through the DITLO, we've shown them how they can be successful, and we've put them in the context that encourages their success. Now we have to see how they rise when the standard is raised. This is where we apply pressure—not as punishment, but as opportunity. Pressure is what turns alignment into action, and how we give people the chance to prove to themselves (and to us) that they can stand strong and deliver at a higher level.

This is where we have an honest conversation. We sit down and say, "Here's what we see in you. Here's how we've realigned your role around your fire. Now, we're going to push you, because I'm confident you can do it when you're working in your strength. Do I have your permission to challenge you now that we're aligned on what you're great at?" That kind of clarity turns pressure into partnership.

This is the opposite of what a helicopter owner would do. Where a helicopter owner holds up employees who aren't holding themselves up, we are allowing our employees to prove that they can function independently and diligently. If they aren't willing to live up to these standards, this isn't the company for them. In business, the motto to live by is coach up or coach out. As Jacob M. Engel put it, "The philosophy of coaching up or out tells everyone, 'We are a meritocracy and we appreciate and applaud you for your positive contribution, *and* we don't believe it helps anyone by holding on to people that either aren't able or willing to move up.'"

Let's revisit my head of marketing, Lucinda. When I saw how she was misusing her time, I realized the situation called for drastic measures, both because of the importance of her position and the severity of the problem. I scheduled multiple one-on-one meetings with her to discuss solutions. Ultimately, I decided to adjust her responsibilities (without docking her pay) based on the things she was confident in, creating an entirely new role. I also gave her tips and tools to be proficient at the job. Now, I was sure she would be successful. I told her to execute on the things she knew how to do, and we'd check back thirty days later. But at that check-in, we were back in the same spot. She didn't do it. She fell short again. And so (coach up or coach out), we let her go.

Lucinda was awesome. I liked her. I knew that she was smart enough and capable enough to do what we were asking her to do. And yet she didn't do it. Why? It wasn't her intelligence or attitude. She was operating at a different level of leadership than what the role required. At her last company, a massive global organization, her job was to maintain a small part of a much larger system. She didn't have to create or optimize anything. She just had to keep her piece of the puzzle running. But in our company, we needed a builder. Someone who could take ownership of an entire function, design the systems, and then drive them forward. She had never been asked to do that before, and when the pressure was applied, she broke.

That's what Crystallizing does. It offers the chance for the employee to soar, using all the help and advice they've been given, supported only by their own ambition and drive. It also offers them a chance to pack up their things and find a job that suits them better. As I like to say, "set people free."

Are those 390 wasted hours still haunting you? Me too. But over the course of the years and years of mistakes and losses, I've found that the 3 Cs are the most effective way to stave off the inefficiencies. When I first started using them, I had to do them pretty frequently, almost once a month. As my team started to learn and as I started to develop procedures to follow, I was able to bump the frequency down to biquarterly. I recommend doing them at least once to twice a year, if not more.

OK, let's recap. We've:

1) Captured our inefficiencies using the time audit.
2) Cultivated a better culture with our employees while giving them the support they need to be productive.
3) Crystallized our employees' new schedules by applying pressure.

We should now be one body of lean schedules and diligent teammates. We have our eyes trained on the prize, and we've cut the distractions. We've talked briefly with our employees about what their responsibilities and schedules will look like. So, now, on to mapping journeys.

CHAPTER 9

Mapping Journeys

If you've seen a few action movies like *Ocean's Eleven* or any of the Avengers movies, chances are you've seen the trope where a team of protagonists comes up with a brilliant plan to beat the antagonist. We watch as the antagonist falls into the traps they lay, each piece coming together to create an unequivocal and satisfying resolution. Then, at the very end, we're left asking the question, *How did they do it? How did they reach this end?* The movie answers the question by taking us back to see how all of the characters worked together to make it happen, each agent pitching in. It almost feels like we're a part of the team, right there alongside everyone as they do their part. Almost. The problem, the reason that we don't quite feel like a member of the team, is that we see how it happened in retrospect. We're not seeing the functions of the team in real time; instead, we're left playing catch-up.

You're probably wondering how this applies to business. In a movie, this grand reveal is a good thing. It's the aha moment where we can really appreciate the ingenuity of the characters. In business, however, if our employees are left playing catch-up, they will feel disjointed with the rest of the company.

Sometimes, what employees need is to see how their jobs fit into the overall process of the company as a whole. Picture a basketball team. If every player is trained only on their position and doesn't understand how the plays work as a whole, they'll probably get by for a while. But sooner or later, someone will miss a rotation on defense or cut the wrong way on offense. The rest of the team won't know how to adjust, and the player who messed up won't realize the ripple effect of their mistake. Pretty soon, you've got broken plays, missed passes, and a scoreboard that isn't moving in your favor. While each player may be skilled at their role, without the bigger picture in mind, they'll never see how their piece contributes to the win. It's the same in business: if your team only knows their isolated responsibilities, they might function for a while, but eventually a small misstep will snowball into the business equivalent of a turnover.

My husband and I created a tool that allows your team to come together to minimize turnovers and maximize points on the board. It's one of the most powerful and yet simple tools that we use in our businesses because it brings many of the tools we've already talked about in this book together into one place. It has saved us countless hours on countless fronts: from the hiring and onboarding of new employees to the delivery of the finished product. I give you the *process map*.

Process Map

The process map is a visual representation of the processes that happen throughout the company. It's a bird's-eye view; a broad look at the way the entire company functions. It's like a road map: at the most zoomed out view, it shows the origin, the destination, and a few stops along the way. When you zoom in, you see each leg of the journey and the twists and turns along that section. The typical journey in a company could look like a section for marketing, then sales, then customer onboarding, then product fulfillment, and finally, offboarding.

Imagine conducting an orchestra. When you look at the whole orchestra, the sounds of the individual parts fall away, leaving one unified piece. On the other hand, you could narrow your perspective down a bit. If you were to focus on one section of instruments, maybe the strings, you would notice how much depth and richness they add. You would also notice if something was wrong, if an instrument was out of tune (we'll come back to that in a minute). This is the power of the process map. It gives you a detailed yet versatile view of the processes within your company – you can zoom in where you want.

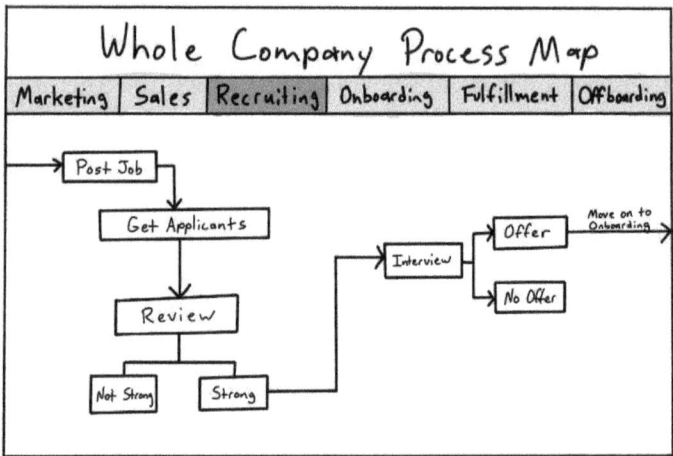

The Customer's Journey

At the most zoomed-out view of your company's process map, you'll see the customer's journey. You see how the company first attracts the customer and then sells the customer. Then you have the actual product fulfillment. This could look like performing a service, delivering a SaaS product, cleaning a house, or maintaining a property. Or maybe it's a physical product that you sell.

This section is useful for showing employees what the whole process looks like and where they fit into the journey. Not only is it helpful to see what role the people around them play, but it's also nice to see what they're really a part of. It can give them a greater sense of purpose. I'm sure you've heard this parable before: three brick layers are hard at work. When asked what he's doing, the first one says, "I'm laying bricks." The second one says, "I'm feeding my family." And the third one? "I'm building a grand cathedral!" Show your employees the cathedral. (In the next chapter, we'll dive into *Future Framing* and go into this in more detail.)

Legs of the Trip

Next, with a process map, you can also zoom in on a specific department to get a clearer picture of one aspect of your business. You should be able to see the beginning, middle, and end of a department's involvement with the workflow. If we zoom in on product fulfillment, for example, we can see where the customer gets passed to them, what actions the customer goes through in that phase, and how they'll be passed on to the next.

A view like this helps remind team members of what their process should look like, and how it affects other processes within the company. As time goes on, people tend to stray from the beaten path. A process map helps get your people back on track. Just like we created Microplays to standardize doing small tasks, creating a process map standardizes the entire journey.

Turns Along the Way

If we look at the process map just a little bit closer, we'll be able to see the specific tasks that need to be completed to reach the milestones within each department. If we are zoomed in on the sales department, tasks could look like reaching out to the customer, having the customer sign documents, or giving them their new customer gift. If you've been paying attention, then you probably know what comes next: the Microplays for each of these tasks are linked. 1 Layer Deep™. This makes it so simple that someone who has never worked with your company before can handle a basic day without any assistance from anyone.

Zooming in to this level is helpful for both the employees and the managers in these departments. From here, the manager can assign tasks based on what needs to be done next and who is available to do it. Once assigned a task, all an employee has to do is open the process map, and they'll find the Microplay for their task linked.

When we create the process map, this also gives us the opportunity to evaluate what tasks we are still having humans do that don't have to be done by humans. What processes can we automate? Are we still having a human send out emails that are the same every time we send them? We can save money and resources on things like this by turning them into what I call Standard Automated Procedures or SAPs, leveraging technology to save money and/or get our employees onto more productive work.

Drawing the Map

So, how do you create a process map? To start, create the process map by using the same time audits we discussed in the previous chapter.

Most business owners follow the same storyline when they incorporate the time audit within their company: First, they have a utopian idea of their process and their employees. All of the employees will be 1oo percent efficient at all times. Then, the business owner does a time audit, and surprise! Santa isn't real. If you've already done the time audit since we talked about it, then you know exactly what I'm talking about. But there is a solution, a way to rebuild the shattered dream.

Once your time audit is done, take that new information and analyze it. A lot of the inefficiency can probably be blamed on the individual; they can definitely go faster, but they didn't realize that they needed to. On the other hand, even with the employees working to their reasonable capacity, they are not going to be able to reach the level of efficiency that we envisioned at the start. This is something we need to account for when we create the process map. We take this new insight and create a new standard procedure that is both more optimal and more reasonable. Now you'll have a new vision that is doable, and there are no excuses for not sticking to it.

This is part of Delete, or *cutting the B.S.* In this case, there's a couple layers of B.S.—your expectations, and the inefficiencies of others. The truth is somewhere between. Find it, set the standard, and get on toward continuous improvement.

Knowing Your Employees

Sound like a lot to throw at your employees? Surprisingly, no. A process map shows the whole picture, the end goal, and how each individual fits into it, but it's still a bird's-eye view, simple and visually appealing. Most employees appreciate how easily it explains such a complex journey.

Plus, they'll remember it. Studies have shown that using visuals enhances retention of information, and many people identify as visual learners. We need to move away from using primarily text-based documents and move towards a more inclusive and versatile format (like our TikTok-ification of SOP's). The process map is a huge step in that direction, plus, it caters to all different styles of learning and retention: You can read the text of the Microplays associated with tasks. You can also see a visual representation of the processes of the company as a whole. You can scroll around to different departments in the company or interact with the calendars. The process map makes it as easy as possible for our people to know what they need to do and to do it.

Conclusion

By creating the process map, we are creating an environment that encourages success in our employees. We're putting bumpers up so that the wrong things are harder to do and the right things are easier to do. We shouldn't stop altering the environment there, though (and no, I'm not talking about the Earth's environment). I'm talking about changing our own environment, or at least our own future. I'm talking about setting ourselves up to be as successful as possible. Or at least I will be talking about that in the next chapter.

∧∧∧

CHAPTER 10

Future Frame

By now you've done the heavy lifting with time audits, DITLOs, Microplays, Gameplans, and Owner Playbooks. You've seen how Align, Delete, Execute clears the fog for your team. This last chapter is where we point all of that inward and make it stick. Not just for the business, but for you.

The two questions now are simple but carry significant weight to them: One, "How do I not lose *steam*?" and two, "How do I not lose *focus*?" If you can answer those, this won't be another "shelf help" book; you'll go through an evolution within yourself to apply it, turn it into habit, make it your culture, and live it.

People love to talk down on "the hustle," and I get it. If you're grinding away at the wrong things, it's miserable and exhausting. But when you're working in your fire, it doesn't feel like hustle. It feels like pure momentum. The work starts giving back more than it takes. That's what we're after here.

Consider Roald Amundsen's race to the South Pole in 1911. Both he and Captain Scott shared the same goal: to get there first. But Amundsen's clarity was razor-sharp. He pared down his team, embraced Inuit techniques (sled dogs, furs, simple diet) and retreated when weather made the push dangerous. Every decision was guided by one thing: the safest, most effective path to the goal. He reached the Pole, turned around, and made it home in one piece.

Scott, on the other hand, had other priorities. Scientific equipment, traditional British decorum, ponies instead of dogs, wool clothing instead of furs. It all slowed him down. He reached the Pole weeks later, but the return trip proved fatal for him and his team.

Amundsen's expedition made his conquest about clarity, focus, preparation, and execution under pressure. He owned his path without shame or ambiguity. That's the core of a Future Frame. It's stripping everything back to the single most important thing and accepting that everything else might need to step aside to achieve that goal.

If you only shape the business, the rest of your life drags you off course. So, we're going to build a Future Frame: a practical progression that keeps the wheels under you and keeps the business moving in the same direction. We'll run it on two tracks: business and personal. Because if you only fix one, the other will pull you off course:

- **Friction**: what's holding you back? In business, it's bottlenecks or misaligned roles. In life, it's overcommitment, guilt, or that 2 a.m. *Am I enough?* voice.

- **Focus**: where you're creating value right now. For the company, it's where the biggest impact happens. For you, it's how you show up as parent, partner, builder.

- **Fire**: what drives you. For the business, it's the mission everyone feels behind. For you, it's the "Why" in showing up for your marriage, your kids, your bold decisions.

- **Frame**: how you move forward with absolute clarity and conviction. You know what matters most, and you move hard on that.

This is a personal inflection point, as much as a business one. Some hard conversations will be owed with daily alignment. Some things, and people, will have to step aside: intentional detachment from what doesn't serve you. It's not simple or easy, but there's speed on the other side. You begin making the right decisions without fear, opportunity compounds, and for the first time, you're not everything to everybody. What you get back is clarity.

This is Future Framing: a structure to live inside so when the noise gets loud and the path gets steep, you keep moving with honesty, alignment, and absolute intention toward what matters most. One. Layer. Deep.

Friction: What's Holding You Back

Friction is the drag that keeps you from moving the way you're meant to. In business, it looks like bottlenecks, wasted effort, or someone sitting in a role that doesn't really match their strengths. In your personal life, it shows up as unclear expectations, saying yes when you should've said no, or the imposter syndrome that whispers "you're not good enough."

The problem with friction is that we get used to it. We start treating misalignment like it's normal. That's why people stay in jobs that drain them or that overcommitment that keeps running you ragged. They don't actually move the needle, but we sum it up with "that's just life." But friction isn't normal. It's the equivalent of driving with the emergency brake half on. You'll keep moving, but it's slower, harder, and eventually something burns out.

That's why the time audit and the DITLO matter so much. They don't just show you inefficiencies; they show you misalignment. They uncover where people are working outside their fire, or where you're carrying a weight that doesn't belong to you. Once you see it, you can deal with it. Do you delete it, delegate it, or redesign it?

Friction isn't failure. It's feedback. It's a signal that something's off track, whether it's in the company or at home. When you start facing it honestly, you'll realize most of the pressure you've been feeling isn't from the size of your goals, it's from the drag of misalignment.

Focus: Where You're Creating Value Right Now

Once you've named the friction, the next step is to get honest about your focus. Focus is where you *currently* create the most value. Not someday, not when everything lines up perfectly, but right now. It's a transitional state of progress, not a permanent one. Focus is the vehicle you can rely on in this season. It's what carries you and the company forward while your vessel is being built, your fire.

This is where intention starts to take shape. In the 1 Layer Deep™ method, once we've created alignment on what's holding us back, we move to intention: deliberately choosing where to put our energy. Focus is the first piece of intention on getting clear on where your contribution actually moves the needle *today*.

In business, this looks like the specific areas where your work is producing outcomes now. Maybe you're the one closing sales because no one else on the team has as high of a close rate as you *right now*. Maybe you're maintaining client relationships or keeping systems stable so the whole thing doesn't fall apart *right now*. Personally, it might be the daily roles you can't outsource *right now*, like the parent keeping routines steady for the kids, the spouse showing up to make home life feel more connected, or the leader making sure decisions don't stall out.

See what's happening? *Right now* is a transitional state. It serves a purpose, but it's not where you're meant to live forever. These aren't small things; they're the very roles that keep everything else from breaking apart.

The key is remembering that focus isn't forever. Just because you're carrying the load *right now* doesn't mean you're stuck there. It's a vehicle you use in the season, because it gives you traction, but it should never become your vessel. When you lean into Focus fully, it gives you traction. It keeps the wheels turning and momentum building, and it creates the space for your true fire to emerge.

Life should be riding on smooth rails. Friction drags you down, but when you're working inside your focus, you've got a track that carries you forward with less resistance. It might not yet be the express line you ultimately want, but it's steady, it's reliable, and it builds momentum. The more you lean into that focus, the faster you move, and the faster you move, the sooner you'll have the capacity to pour yourself into the fire that truly fuels you.

Fire: What Drives You

Fire is different from focus. Focus is what carries you *right now*. Fire is what makes you want to throw off the covers in the morning, jump out of bed, and run straight at it. It's not duty. It's not an obligation. It's that pull inside of you that doesn't need to be forced; the deepest sense of drive that compels you to move forward with fearlessness, unphased by uncertainty of *"what if."*

In business, fire is the mission people can feel. Hitting numbers might keep the lights on, but fire is what makes the work matter. It's the difference between having a job and having a purpose. Your team doesn't just clock in and out when they feel that fire. They show up invested when they know they're part of something bigger.

In your personal life, Fire is why you keep saying yes to the hard things. It's why you fight to show up for your kids even when you're tired, why you keep investing in your marriage when it would be easier to coast, why you walk into a real estate deal or a bold move in your business when fear keeps telling you that it's safer to wait and play it safe. Fire is what gets you to stand back up when friction throws you off balance.

Florence Nightingale had that kind of fire. When she walked into the Crimean War hospitals, she didn't walk into glory; she walked into hell. The scene was unbearable. Rows of soldiers crammed into filthy wards, lying in their own waste, infection killing more soldiers than bullets ever did. Nearly half of the men who entered those hospitals never came out.

Most accepted it as the cost of war. Florence didn't. She couldn't. Where others saw inevitability, she saw preventable death. That conviction burned so deeply in her that she refused to let "normal" stand, pushing her past the excuses. She scrubbed the floors herself and demanded changes no one thought possible. She forced the institution of sanitation. The result was staggering: because of her, mortality rates fell from over 40 percent to just 2 percent. Not because she had rank, or wealth, or advanced medicine, but because she carried something most others didn't: the unshakable conviction that things could be different. She didn't wait for permission, and she didn't back down when the resistance came. She stood in the filth and chaos and held to that belief. Then she made things different.

That's the nature of fire. It doesn't settle. It's the conviction that refuses to bow to think, *That's just how it is.* Fire is the drive that transforms fear into fuel, and it's what will carry you when focus alone isn't enough. And when others catch sight of that conviction, it doesn't just change you, it changes them, too. That's where intention turns into energy. Fearlessness shows up here. Not because fear is gone, but because what's driving you is stronger than what's trying to stop you.

Frame: Where to Go from Here

Frame is where the future stops being an idea and becomes action. This is where you swallow your pride, shake off the doubt, and put one foot in front of the other with conviction. Everything we've built so far - stripping away friction, leaning into focus, uncovering your fire - comes to nothing if you don't frame it with execution.

Most people stall here. They treat the future like a *"someday"* project. They leave this step abstract, vague, or aspirational. But Frame isn't about inspiration, it's about traction. It's the point where you draw your future self into today and start acting as if you're already there. Because if you don't, you'll drift back into the exact same place you were before you picked up this book. Overcommitted, misaligned, and frustrated that nothing changes.

Think of the way cathedral builders worked in the Middle Ages. Many of them knew they would never live to see the final spire rise into the sky. Yet they laid their stones with precision anyway, carving details into beams that would sit a hundred feet above the ground where no human eye would ever see them. Why? Because the frame mattered. Because their part, no matter how small or unseen, made the structure hold. Generations later, those cathedrals still stand, simply because someone picked up a chisel and executed the work, one intentional cut at a time.

That's the essence of Frame. It isn't glamorous or about proving anything to anyone, but putting clear stakes in the ground and saying: *This is what I'm executing on. This is how I'm showing up. This is the structure that will hold me to it.* The frame keeps this work from being a *"shelf helper"* you read once and makes it a lifestyle. It's the purest form of honesty you can give yourself and your team to live with alignment, have clear intention, and execute on what matters most. 1 Layer Deep™.

The Finished Frame

Future Framing isn't complicated. It's four sides of a structure that holds you steady when things get loud:

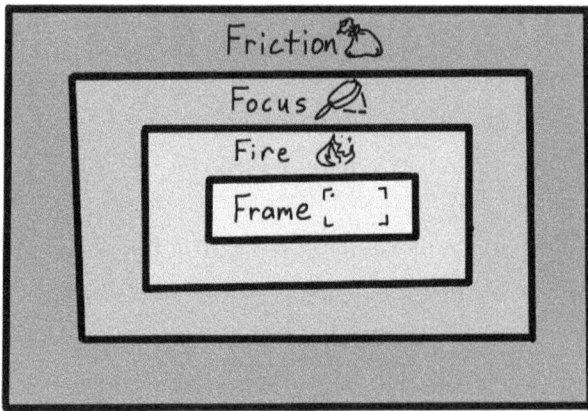

- **Friction**: seeing what's dragging you down and calling it for what it is.
- **Focus**: knowing where you create value *right now* and leaning into it fully.
- **Fire**: the conviction that gets you out of bed in the morning, that deeper "why" that doesn't need to be forced.
- **Frame**: locking it in with execution so the future pulls from "someday" to today.

When you lay all four down, you build a structure that keeps you honest, aligned, and intentional. 1 Layer Deep™.

A finished Frame doesn't have to be complicated. It isn't a 40-page strategy deck that nobody reads. It's more like a DITLO for your future self. Just like when we sit down with a team member and walk through how their day actually plays out, a Frame takes everything you've uncovered: your friction, your focus, your fire, and turns it into a picture of where you're headed.

For yourself, that means writing down what life looks like when you're aligned and intentional. What does a day look like when you're showing up in your fire? How do you start the morning? Where do you put your energy? Who's alongside you? You don't need paragraphs of fluffy language. A couple of pages that make you feel it when you read it back is enough. Think of it as a playbook you can return to, not a vision statement you frame on the wall.

For your team, delivery matters. A Future Frame isn't meant to overwhelm them; it's meant to ground them. The same way we deliver DITLO presentations with simple, visual, human elements, your Frame should show them where you're going in a way they can connect to. A few pages, some visuals, even photos or screenshots that capture the feeling of where you're headed. When they hear it, they should be able to see themselves in it: "Here's where we're headed. Here's how your role connects. Here's what it feels like when we get there."

That's the power of a finished Frame. It brings the future close. It gives you and your team something to align around that isn't abstract, but practical. And it keeps you from drifting back to "someday" thinking. The Frame is a tool you can use, over and over again, to keep yourself and your company 1 Layer Deep™. Aligned, intentional, and executing on what matters most.

Carrying It Forward

You've reached the end of this book, but really, this is where the work begins. The question now is simple: **how do you keep going?** How do you stay aligned when life tries pulling you back?

This is where 1 Layer Deep™ becomes more than a method. Over time, it becomes a mindset you practice, then a culture, and ultimately a lifestyle. It works its way into daily alignment with your team and your family through intentional conversations. It makes hard choices about what (and who) you leave behind because it doesn't serve where you're headed. It brings intention in how you show up as a parent, partner, and builder. And it creates execution without the need for validation on what matters most.

Don't take this as theoretical. I've had to live this out in my own life. It meant leaving circles of people I cared about because they weren't aligned with where I needed to go, my greater purpose. It meant saying no to things I could do well so I could say yes to the things only I could do. And what I found on the other side was incredible clarity, speed, and abundance of opportunity that compounded in ways I never imagined.

The same is possible for you. Keep practicing 1 Layer Deep™. Create Alignment, push for Intentional clarity, and lock in on what you need to Execute. You won't drift back into "someday." You'll keep moving with conviction toward the future you want to live.

I can't wait to see what you create.

1LD90 BUSINESS GAMEPLAN
A Note from Me to You

I don't want this to be another book that ends up on your shelf, collecting dust. You know the cycle, read, highlight, get inspired... and then nothing changes.

That's why I created the **1LD90 Gameplan.**

This is a free tool I built just for you. It's not more theory. It's a ninety-day, step-by-step Gameplan that takes everything in this book and helps you *install it* into your business in minutes a day.

Here's how it works:

- **Days 1–30:** Spend 5-15 minutes capturing quick wins and writing your first Microplays.
- **Days 31–60:** Invest 10-15 minutes linking Microplays into Gameplans and aligning your team.
- **Days 61–90:** Dedicate 15-20 minutes to building your first Owner Playbook and embedding rhythms that scale.

Not heavy. Not overwhelming. Just enough time to feel real, without tipping into too much. And those minutes compound. By day ninety, you'll have an operating system that makes your business lighter, clearer, and easier to run without you carrying the whole thing on your back.

This book gives you the frameworks. The **1LD90 Gameplan** gives you the free tool to actually put them into action. For more tools and resources visit 1layerdeep.com/resources

You don't just get to say, "I read this book for my business." You'll be able to say, "I run it 1 Layer Deep™."

1LD90

Check The Box
Micro Moves for Massive Change

START YOUR 90-DAY GAMEPLAN

1	2	3	4	5	6	7	8	9	10
11	12	13	14	15	16	17	18	19	20
21	22	23	24	25	26	27	28	29	30
31	32	33	34	35	36	37	38	39	40
41	42	43	44	45	46	47	48	49	50
51	52	53	54	55	56	57	58	59	60
61	62	63	64	65	66	67	68	69	70
71	72	73	74	75	76	77	78	79	80
81	82	83	84	85	86	87	88	89	90

ACKNOWLEDGMENTS

To my parents, **Lisa & Jaime Garcia** — thank you for supporting this crazy little girl and always believing in her. Your love, encouragement, and unwavering belief in me made this dream possible.

My Kids

- Billy Morris
- Austin Morris
- Yaya DeLucien

Your support means everything to me. You are my biggest inspiration and the reason I keep pushing forward.

Supported the Journey (Notable Mentions)

- Dan Martell
- Debbie Sardone
- Nicole and Timmy Bauer
- Kayla Fair
- Ashley Peterson

Thank You's (Launch Team)

To my incredible launch team—your energy, enthusiasm, and belief in this project kept me motivated. I'm deeply grateful for each of you:

Alayna Nestman	Ewa Pluciennik	McKenzie Basaldua
Ali Tankersley	Faith Maldonado Castillo	Meaghan Likes
Amanda Cobb	Faith McLamore Tate	Medard Sotta
Amber Hathaway	Jennifer Garcia	Megan Schmidt
Amy Mays	Jennifer Hudson	Michelle DeLucien
Amy Toppins Belanger	Jennifer Tangeman	Michelle McNiff
Amy Winn Smith	Jess Rockatansky	Michelle Zaklukiewicz Krueger

Andrea Barbagallo

Jhon LeBaron

Molly Moran

Angel Derstler

Kami Waszkiewicz

Monica Garcia

Angela Chanowsky

Kasy Allen

Nichole Love Devescovi

Angela Gammon

Kathy Merchant

Nicole Kalb

Angela McGill Moreno

Katona Lynn Zito

Olivia Bray

April Garcia

Kayla Bittick

Pam Clyde

Ashley Rena Russell

Kayla Terry

Pamela Parker Northcutt

Ashley Williams

Kelli Watkins Nance

Patrick Cotroneo

Audra Gorsett

Kelly Klein

Pristine Beers

Beatriz Jorge

Keyli Friday-Prado

Rafaela Assenço

Billie Hayes

Kim Jolley

Raquel Jackson Lindsay

Bre Tschilar	Kris Koenig	Raylene Alicia
Brett Lawrence	Krisia Haag	Renee Dickinson
Carter Dunham	Kristen Prejean	Rita Right
Cassi Taylor	Kristy Cooper	Rose Rogers
Charles Rouse	Lacie Nash	Sandra Henderson
Chelsey Shine	Laura Natoli	Sonia Alvarado Escoto
Cheryl Diggins	Laurel Chiakas	Stacey Rose
Christina Thomas	Leah Hennigar Munroe	Staci R Vega
Cindy Alcantar	Leah Mtegha	Stephanie Wilson Scott
Clean 2 Shine, LLC	Lilly Perez	Summer Carothers Abram
Cory Bittick	Lindsay Ryan-Buck	Susan Stocker
Cristina Thomas	Lisa Clayton Siciliano	Tami Sellers

Crystal Stolzer	Lisa Fulton Garcia	Tammy Holmes
Danit Cheistwer	Lisa Kirkpatrick	Tavana Brown
Dani Duke	Lisa Pane Ciao	Taylor Krueger
Darryl L Jackson	Lorinda Beck	Taylor Loethen
Dee Charvat	Lynnette Malone	Taylor Matthews
Donna Garman	Marisa Perera-Garcia	Tetiana Kolcheva
Drew Larison	Marsy Lucena	Tiffany Welch
Erica Lefler	Martha Woodward	Tracy Palma
Erika Perez	Marvin Salcido	Vanessa Higgins

Employees: 1LD | WootRecruit | Organize It | Sell Convert Clean Team

- Miguel De Leon
- Eliani Solorzano
- Rexie Sumagaysay
- Rigo Villeda
- Maria Musa
- Marilyn Suazo
- Alfredo Molina
- William Palma
- Rico Donato
- Gabriela Mejia
- Jayden Campbell
- Marsy Lucena
- Gabriela Moran

ABOUT THE AUTHOR

Libby DeLucien is a systems strategist, founder, and unapologetically practical business builder. She's the CEO of WootRecruit, Sell Convert Clean & Organize It, and creator of the 1 Layer Deep™1 Layer Deep™ Method. After scaling her own cleaning company into a multi-location powerhouse and launching one of the leading recruiting platforms for home service businesses, Libby became known for helping founders escape the day-to-day by building businesses that run without them. Through her 1 Layer Deep™ method and stage talks across the country, she's taught thousands of entrepreneurs how to reclaim their time, lead with clarity, and finally stop being the bottleneck. She's a mom, wife, and truth-teller who believes real success is when you can leave for weeks and nothing breaks.